MASTER CUT GOLDEN BAR

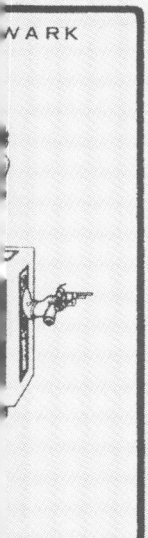

MISS WOODBINE

MR. STAR

ADVERTISING COLLECTABLES

KEITH & PENNY GRETTON
BBR PUBLISHING

All rights reserved. No part of this publication may be reproduced, stored in any retrieval system, or transmitted in any form or by any means, electronic, mechanical, photocopying or otherwise without the prior permission in writing of the publishers.

Published by BBR Publishing, 2 Strafford Avenue, Elsecar, Nr Barnsley, S Yorks, S74 8AA, England.

ISBN 0 9508484 5 X Advertising Collectables (hardback only)

Copyright © Keith and Penny Gretton
First published in 1989

Keith Gretton 1990

Typeset in England by John Mackie, Burton on Trent, Staffs. Printed in Scotland by Bookmag, Inverness.

To Mark and Simon whose tolerance and co-operation we have appreciated even though we do not always appreciate them.

ACKNOWLEDGEMENTS

We wish to thank all those who gave us encouragement, information and photographs, as well as those who generously loaned some of their most prized pieces. No one said no. We are especially indebted to the late Michael Franklin who contributed so much to the history of biscuit tins and hope more collectors of advertising will, in the same way, share their discoveries, adding to everyone's enjoyment of a fascinating subject.

Our special thanks go to:–

Mike and Pam Ball
Steve Burton
Henry Chesterman
Christie's, South Kensington
Lena Cooke
Andrew Cunningham
Bob and Sue Davidson
Simon and Sally Dray
Tony Durrant
Lembit Eha
John England
Judith Fisher
Rob Gee
Rob and Kath Goodacre
John Hall
Gary Higgins
Brian Howes
Norman Lewis

Roy Morgan
Godfrey Omar-Parsons
Robert Opie
Colin Read
Alan Redgate
Dave Rogers
Jeff Small
Mike Smith
Sotheby's, Chester
Nick Southall
Nev Summers
Colin Tetley
Bez Turner
Herbert Uedelhoven
Robert Vince
Brian Wagstaff
Don Widdowfield
Keith Wilson

and the late Warner Cooke, one of those many artists without whom the Festival of Britain and all that followed could not have happened.

THE AUTHORS

PENNY GRETTON

Born in London in 1948 to commercial artist parents. Trained at the Architectural Association and qualified as an architect. Now has two children, a dilapidated Victorian house full of 'things' and no spare time.

KEITH GRETTON

I still have strong childhood memories of that time when all shops seemed to have expensive mahogany counters and most purchases were weighed or counted and wrapped and groceries were delivered weekly, bread three times a week and milk twice a day.

While at Stafford College of Art I visited the Festival of Britain and experienced the dramatic change which modern design coupled with increased prosperity brought about.

After more than a decade as an antiques market and old bottle show stallholder, I now have a shop unit specialising in old advertising. I have contributed to British and foreign collectors' magazines and give lectures on British advertising art and packaging to anyone who will listen. According to Penny I am always buying myself presents as most of all I still enjoy collecting.

PRICE GUIDE

(A) _____ under   £   2

(B) _____ under   £   5

(C) _____ under   £ 10

(D) _____ £ 10 - £ 25

(E) _____ £ 25 - £ 50

(F) _____ £ 50 - £ 100

(G) _____ £ 100 - £ 200

(H) _____ £ 200 plus

The prices quoted are for items in very good or mint condition and not all as portrayed in the photographs. Ceramic must be mint with strong transfer printing but a little rusting round the fixing holes on enamel signs is acceptable and figures may have an amount of judicious repainting. Rusting, fading and scratching on printed tin reduce the value considerably and glass should show no sign of 'sickness.' Paper and card should also be mint but obviously packets and boxes will have been opened.

Any antique or collectable is worth only what the purchaser is willing to pay and the seller is willing to accept which leaves a considerable margin round the prices given in any guide.

CONTENTS

INTRODUCTION 8 - 9

STREET SCENE 10 - 23
Wooden crates, vehicles, enamel signs, thermometers, glass tablets, letters and symbols, fire marks, posters.

POINT OF SALE 24 - 59
Figures, lights, showcards, tin signs, dispensers, display pieces, condiment pots, ashtrays, matchbox stands, match strikers, trays, coasters, measures.

PACKAGING 62 - 95
Tins, vestas, matchboxes, boxes, packets, wrapping paper, labels, milk bottle tops, milk bottles, bottles, storage jars, pots.

PROMOTIONALS 96 - 113
Games, games markers, playing cards, bookmarks, inkwells, office supplies, pocket mirrors, bottle openers, calendars, postcards, shoe horn & button hooks, badges & medallions, pottery.

OTHER EPHEMERA 114 - 117
Inserts, mechanicals, billheads.

INTRODUCTION

Victorian signs arranged like paintings and ornaments in a Victorian drawing room; richly crowded and competing for attention. (*Illustration from 'The 20th Century Business Book', edited by Walter Grierson.*)

Although seventeenth and eighteenth century posters and trade cards can still be found, the most entertaining and attractive advertising collectables date from the nineteenth century when the industrial revolution caused all the changes necessary to produce a consumer society.

Serviced by the railway developments of the 1830's the Victorian economic boom in the 1860's established styles and forms of packaging, promotion and display which were to remain basically unchanged for almost a century. Britain became a nation of shopkeepers, not in the grand style of imperial rulers, but small and domestic in scale like the villages from which the industrial workers came.

Without any qualms, manufacturers borrowed, bought or plagiarised fine art for their advertising imagery: Landseer's 'Monarch of the Glen' emphasised the Scottishness of Dewar's whisky while Millais' 'Bubbles' blew his pipe for Pear's. Sentimental, genre and quasi-religious paintings were reproduced to give respectability by association to the grocery trade just as banks used greco-roman façades to symbolise their rational, solid and enduring status.

Traditional engravers and printers were overtaken by changing demands and innovations in technology and a new generation of largely anonymous graphic designers and illustrators intermixed old and invented new typefaces, ignored academic rules of composition and drawing, distorting proportions and perspective in order to produce strong images with clear messages. The results were often charmingly naïve but their approach is significantly echoed in modern art of the twentieth century. The underlying motivation behind fine and commercial art is different but their interaction and relationship during the last hundred years helps to illustrate many collectors' fascination with old advertising.

In 1913, Apollinaire wrote that Picasso and Braque incorporated letters in some of their pictures "because label, notice and advertisement play a very important aesthetic role in the modern city and are well suited for incorporation into works of art." Later that decade Kurt Schwitters took more than the letters of advertising and produced collages of tickets, cheese wrappers and cigar bands, honouring their existence by giving them a place in his art. However, the actual design of advertising material was not then a proper subject for the fine artist and many of the academic painters who did produce commercial art used pseudonyms to protect their reputations.

In the 1950's a retailing revolution began to produce self-service supermarket chains which outgrew the domestic scale of the small shop. Even the giant C.W.S. organisation lost its pre-eminence because it did not respond quickly enough to the changing ethos. Supermarkets developed the simplified style of post war graphic design to obtain a generic image for their own brand goods and the jewel like complexity of packaging design so suited to the small shop began to disappear.

In the aftermath of the Second World War people had demanded change, a brave new world in which the remnants of Victoriana were reviled, but soon a new generation was to look back more sympathetically to the past. Pop Art was born out of the conflict between this youthful nostalgia and the modernist style and chose the icons of advertising for its subject matter.

British artists like Peter Blake and Bruce Lacey used the advertising idioms of the corner shop and the workman's cafe as a landscape of reference for their art. In America, Andy Warhol and James Rosenquist, who both had backgrounds in commercial art, joined painters like Jasper Johns in a movement which isolated single images of mass culture and re-presented them as art.

In the interplay of commercial and fine art, Pop Art produced two different reactions. Some advertisers who had been employing glossy and sophisticated imagery chose to return to a stronger, more direct style similar to Pop Art, while others explored the potential of sharp focus photography, moving away from the painted image altogether. Now fine art exploits the techniques and technologies developed for commercial purposes and artists who have shared the same formal training continue a dialogue and more easily exchange roles.

Some collectors of old advertising may be or become local historians, sociologists or archaeologists of consumerism but most people will appreciate the decorative appeal of this evolving art form which deals in social icons, the full cultural significance of which only time can judge.

WOODEN CRATES

STREET SCENE

Before radio and television, general advertising centred on the street rather than the home. Every available surface, including the vehicles, was turned into a collage of posters and signs.

Rain washable enamels, so suitable for smoke polluted cities, festooned the railway stations. Along platforms, orange and black slogans might proclaim, "Virol, Good for Children. Good for Invalids. Good for Nursing Mothers. Good for You." While as the train pulled out of the station two men standing transfixed in a field might be seen holding a ladder and cans of Hall's Distemper.

Rolling stock, often owned by the breweries, timber merchants and oil companies, displayed company logos. Free of such blatant advertising, engines and carriages were tastefully restricted to the company name.

Top - QUAKER OATS. Open wooden crate with black printing. c.1930. (32 x 47 x 65 cms) ....(C)

Middle - Front and side views of SUNLIGHT SOAP open wooden crate with black and red printing. Early C20th. (16 x 53 x 40 cms) ....(C)

Bottom - ROBIN STARCH. Lidded wooden crate with brown and red printing and multi-coloured printed paper label on underside of lid. Early C20th. (49 x 32 x 17 cms). Such items are rarely found intact and in fine condition. ....(D)

VEHICLES

At every terminus, on the pavement and stacked high and neat on delivery vans and lorries, wooden crates showed their crisply stamped origins and contents. These simple one, two or three colour printed boxes are close in concept to contemporary supermarket bulk or economy range packs designed as components for multiple stacks.

Reusing opened packing cases for display was an early idea which confectionery manufacturers and pharmacy companies still employ in their more sophisticated folding lid, cardboard boxes. Other crates and boxes had easily removable card tops printed in rich lithographic colours, which could then be used as showcards.

Outdoor advertising is now strictly prescribed in the name of safety and 'good taste'. The opportunities for adornments, such as car radiator caps looking like ships' figureheads, have gone, but Young's Brewery still turns heads with its horse drawn drays and full size, 1912 Model T Ford Matchbox toy look alikes currently deliver real goods.

George Hazel, the dapper station master of Lidd, was reputedly the model for Sharpe's SIR KREEMY KNUT, their hazelnut toffee toff, here seen as a metal radiator cap mounted on wood. Early 1930's. (13 cms high) .... (G)

One of the vehicles lined up in Battersea Park prior to the Veteran Commercial Vehicle London to Brighton run in 1987.

ENAMEL SIGNS

The technique of fusing coloured glass to iron dates from the 1800's but not until 1889 were enamel signs in sufficient demand to cause the Patent Enamel Company Limited to build a factory exclusively devoted to their production. The iron based sign, recognise by its grey washed back, was more rigid with clearer colours than the lighter steel versions introduced in the 1920's, a time when silkscreen printing also began to replace the more exacting processes of stencilling, rubber stamping and applying lithographic transfers.

Millions of enamel signs were made but steel shortages and a change in design ethos in the 1950's ensured their virtual end of production. Only recent demand for reproductions has produced a small resurgence.

Top left - GOSSAGES' SOAP. Black, white, blue, red and yellow. Early C20th. (60 x 31 cms) ....(F)

Middle left - EDWARDS'. Blue, white, yellow, orange, green and black. c.1910. (25.5 x 33 cms) ....(F)

Bottom left - JOHN SMITH. Blue, white and grey. c.1910. (41 x 53 cms) ....(E)

Below - CAPSTAN. Blue, black and white. One of a pair which were often displayed on pavement stands. 1930-50. (46 cms diameter) ....(D)

ENAMEL SIGNS

Above - W H SMITH. Black, white, red, brown, pink and yellow. c.1920's. (40 x 63 cms).....................(F)
Top right - MILLERS. Brown, white, green, black and grey. c.1910. (29.3 x 21.5 cms)......................(E)
Middle right - SMITH'S. Multi-coloured, double-sided. c. 1930. (38 x 51 cms)..(E)
Bottom right - WILLS'S STAR. Brown, orange, green, white and black. c. 1925. (60.5 x 91 cms)(F)
Below - ESSOLUBE. White, blue, green, brown and yellow. 1933. (66 cms diameter)....................(F)

ENAMEL SIGNS

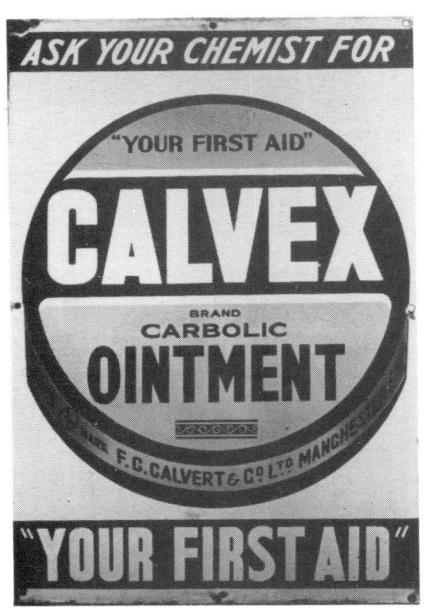

BP ETHYL. Blue, grey, black, orange and white. c.1935. (53 x 61 cms)..(E)

CALVEX. Two tone green on white. c.1930. (50.5 x 76.5 cms)..(E)

TIZER. Black, red and white. c.1935. (30 x 91 cms) ....(D)

Below - REDGATE. Blue, red and white. 1948. (28 x 81.5 cms)..(E)

BP MOTOR SPIRIT pump sign. Red, white and blue. c.1930. (35.5 cms diameter)..................................(F)

ENAMEL SIGNS

Below - TGO. Red, green, black and white. c. 1950. (38 x 56 cms) .... (D)

Right - GOLD FLAKE. Yellow, blue, brown, red, black and white. c.1930. (91.5 x 45.5 cms) .... (F)
Below - MELOX. Black, brown, white, blue and red. c.1930. (45.5 x 66 cms) .... (F)

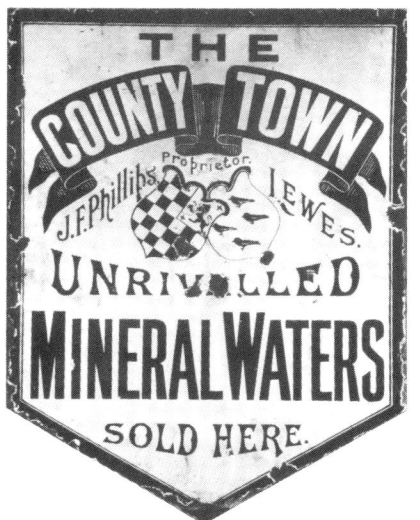

COUNTY TOWN. Double sided, hanging sign. Blue and white. c.1915. (50 cms high) .... (E)

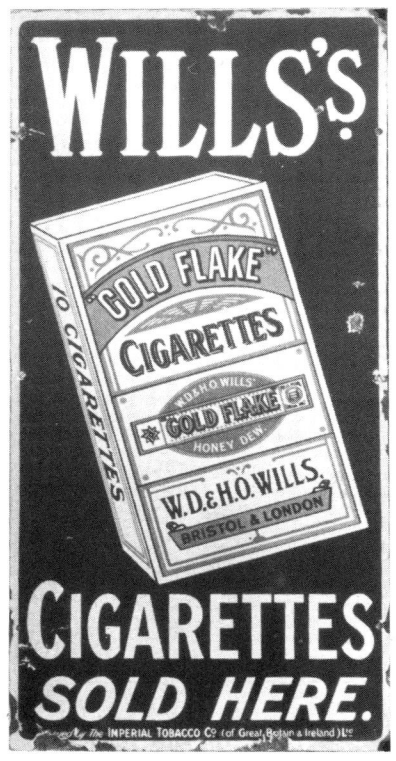

ENAMEL SIGNS

STEPHENS'. Blue, black and white. Early C20th.
(40 x 91 cms) ....(F)

RAJAH. Black, white, red, blue and brown. c.1905.
(46 x 25 cms) ....(G)
Left - WORTHINGTON'S. Red, white and black. c. 1950. (14 x 11.5 cms) ....(D)

STYLE AND WYNCH Brewery. Two tone brown, orange, cream, yellow and grey. c.1925. (35 cms high) ....(G)

ENAMEL SIGNS

Below - PERTH DYE WORKS. Black and white. c.1915. (45 cms high) .... (E)

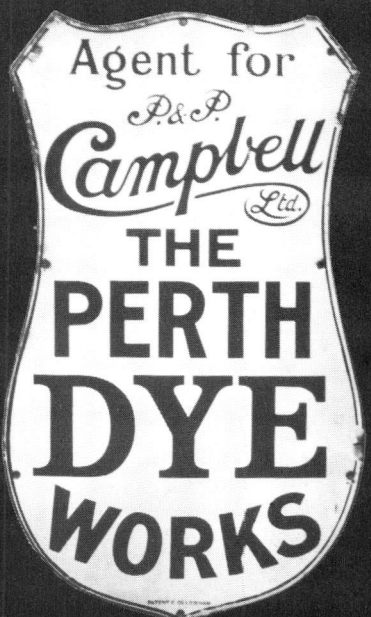

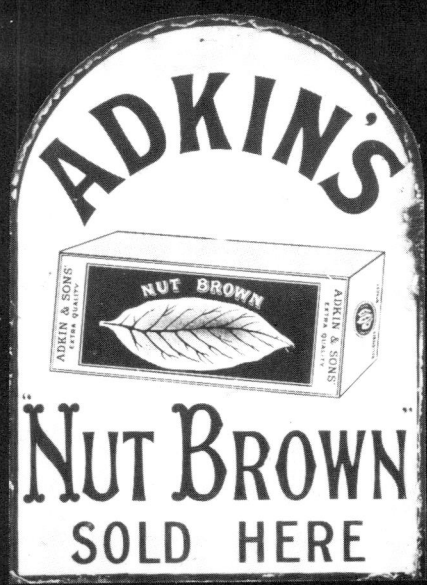

ADKINS. Double sided, side hung. Brown and white. c. 1910. (35.5 x 25 cms) .... (E)

Far right - WILL'S'S. Green on white. c.1930. (15.3 x 61 cms) .... (D)
Middle right - REEVES. Black and white. c.1935. (2 x 52.5 cms) .... (D)
Right - STEPHENS'. Black, white, blue, brown and red. c.1895. (61 x 13 cms) .... (G)
Below - BATTERSEA BOROUGH COUNCIL. Black, red and white. c.1910. (10 x 6.5 cms) .... (B)

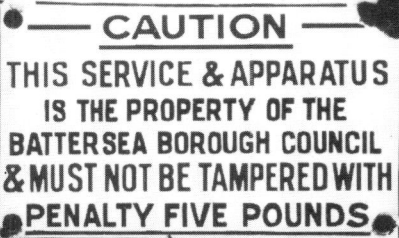

ENAMEL SIGNS

Below - 1d MONSTERS. Black, green, yellow and white. c.1900. (61 x 33 cms) ....(E)

Left - NORTHGATE BEERS. Black, white, blue and red. c.1920. (117 cms diameter) ....(G)

Right - FRY'S COCOA. The price usually displayed on this sign has been enamelled over presumably because of inflation in the 1920's. Blue, black, grey, white, red, yellow and brown. (30.5 cms diameter) ....(D)

ROWNTREE'S. Blue, white, yellow, mauve and turquoise. c.1920. (63.5 x 14 cms) ....(E)

THERMOMETERS

Durable enamelled iron or steel was not only used for signs but outdoor enamel faced clocks, thermometers and barometers, their provision being regarded as a valuable civic amenity. In a country where weather changes are not strongly allied to the season and in a period before weather forecasts and reports, thermometers and barometers attracted keen interest and also proved an ideal vehicle for promotional advertising. In some areas primary school playgrounds displayed giant thermometers courtesy of Stephens' Ink. Barber shops, newsagents and tobacconists were the usual location for others.

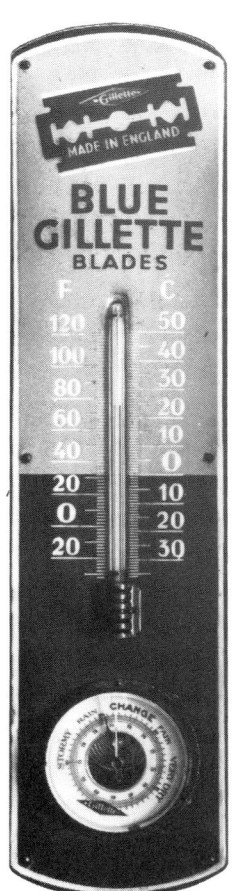
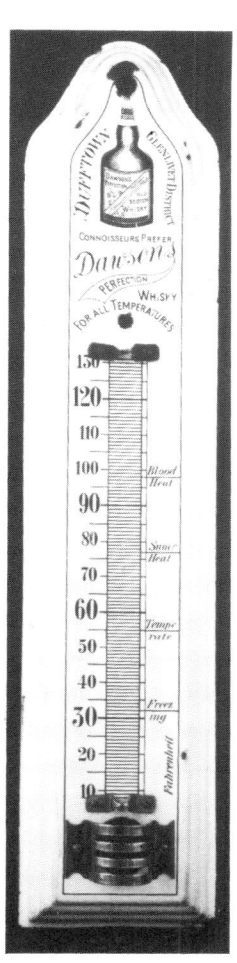
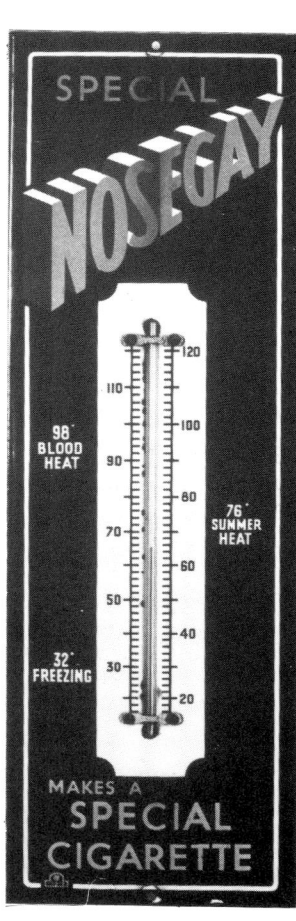

Left - BLUE GILLETTE BLADES thermometer and barometer combined. Two tone blue and white. c.1934. (62 x 15 cms) ....(G)

Middle - DAWSONS WHISKY. Black and white. c.1890's. (41 cms high) .... (F) (G complete with thermometer)

Right - NOSEGAY CIGARETTES. Black, white, red and yellow. c.1930. (57 x 19 cms) ....(F)

GLASS TABLETS

LUCAS. Brilliant Signs Ltd. catalogue illustration. 1939.

TETLEY ALES. Multi-coloured pictorial with black surround and gold letters. c.1950. (28 x 50 cms) .... (E)

Right - GUINNESS. Black, gold lettering and beige, red and black label. c.1950. (28.5 x 51 cms) .... (E)

Some early gilded glass signs were hand painted by signwriters working on the back of the glass, others had letters carved in wood, painted and placed behind glass. Then, in the 1890's, the newly formed Brilliant Signs Company patented new processes. Their slogan, "Advertising efficiency commands commercial success," must have been persuasive as they remained in business until 1975. In the 1930's letters gilded with 23-carat gold leaf could cost £1 each, but, like their "Durasign Tablets", were designed to last.

LETTERS AND SYMBOLS

Above - Red, acrylic, shop fascia letter with metal fixings. Post 1960. (32 cms high) .... (B)
Above right - Mass produced, brass, exterior display letter. Post 1920. (5.6 cms high) .... (B)

Below - YALE key, double sided, hanging sign. Cast metal painted gold with green transfer lettering block. Late 1930's. (78 cms long) .... (F)

The tradesman's figurative hanging symbols designed to guide the illiterate began to disappear in the late eighteenth century when the law of 1792 restricted their size in order to minimize accidents and squeaking.

More general retailing and mass education then heralded the development of lettered fascia boards and the few symbols subsequently made for hanging inside and out merely signified traditional service or displayed a trade mark.

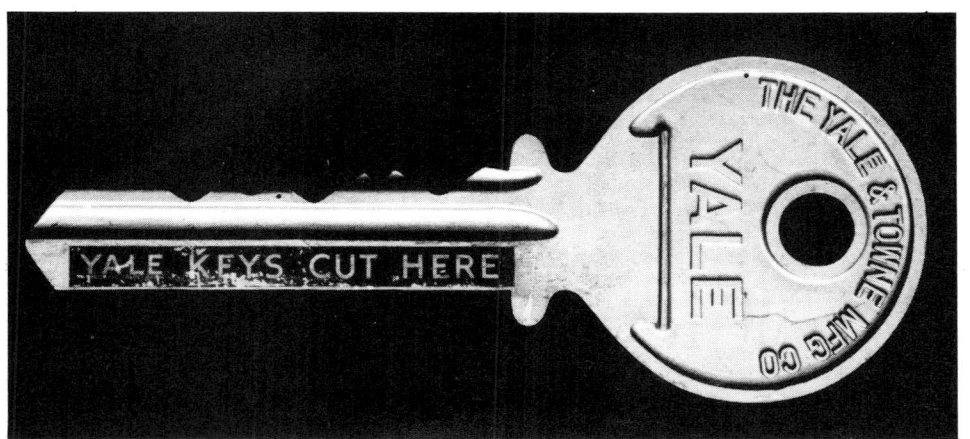

FIREMARKS

First used in 1696, these sometime painted and gilded lead plaques numerically identified then unnumbered buildings for the insurance companies' private fire brigades.

Photograph courtesy of Christie's, South Kensington.

Top row, left to right - SALOP FIRE OFFICE. 1780 - 1890. (19 cms high) (G)   WESTMINSTER FIRE OFFICE. First issued 1717. (24 cms high) (G)   KENT FIRE INSURANCE CO. Earliest Invicta mark issued 1803. (22 cms high) .... (G)

Middle row - HAND IN HAND FIRE OFFICE originally known as the Amicable Contributership. 1696 - 1905. (22 cms high) (G)   ROYAL EXCHANGE. C18th. (21 cms high) (E)   BRISTOL CROWN FIRE OFFICE. C18th. (20 cms high) .... (G)

Bottom row - ROYAL EXCHANGE. C18th. (19 cms high) (E)   BATH FIRE OFFICE. 1767-1827. (22 cms high) (G)   ROYAL EXCHANGE. C18th. (19.5 cms high) .... (E)

POSTERS

Although printed in vast numbers, few old copies of product posters survive, while entertainment and travel, even excluding modern reproductions, are common.

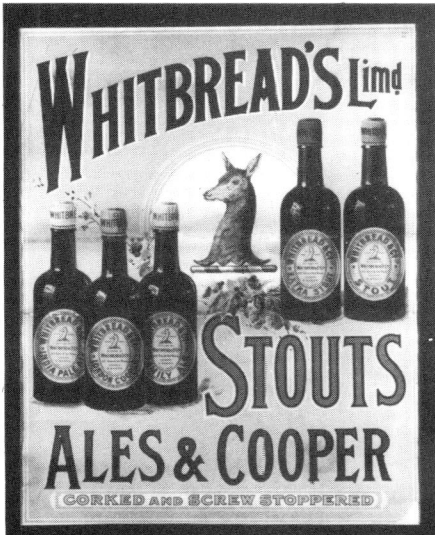

WHITBREAD'S STOUTS. Multi-coloured, chromo lithograph. c.1904. (50 x 65 cms) .... (F)

WISDEN. Multi-coloured lithograph. 1930's. (52 x 40 cms) .... (E)

COBB & CO'S. Multi-coloured lithograph. Pre 1920. (48 x 73.5 cms) .... (F)

FIGURES

POINT OF SALE

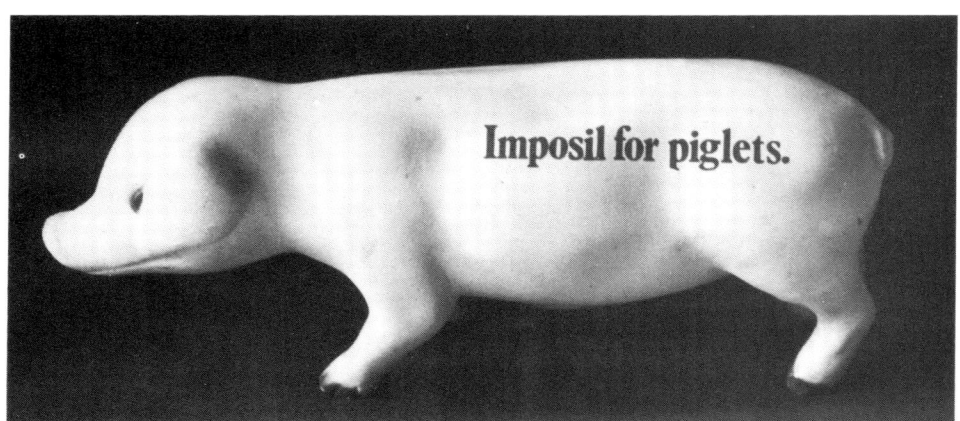

IMPOSIL. Moulded rubber composition painted pink with black transfer lettering. 1950's. (35 cms long) .... (D)

Below left - DR SCHOLL'S ZINO PADS. Ceramic, white and pink with black transfer lettering. Royal Doulton. 1936. (19.5 cms high) .... (F)
Below right - OMNIPED. Moulded rubber composition painted pink, red and black. Late 1930's. (25 cms high) (D)

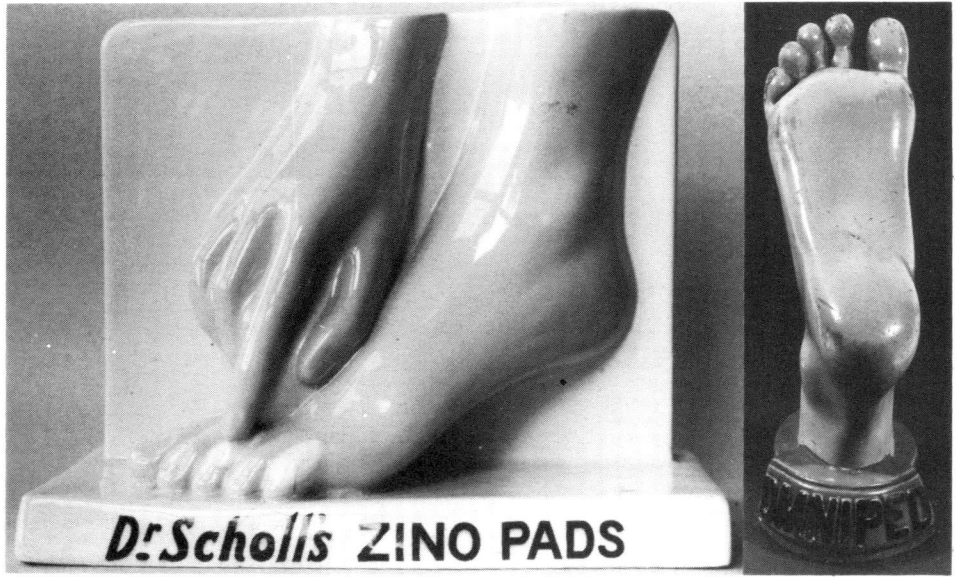

FIGURES

When industrialisation separated manufacturer from retailer, shopkeepers and their customers had to be persuaded to buy branded goods. Producers ensured stockists displayed their merchandise to its best advantage by encouraging the installation of fixtures permanently marked with trade names and by issuing free all kinds of decorative display material.

Rival products battled for attention using life and shelf sized figures, banners and signs, while bar counters were supplied with more discrete reminders applied to functional objects such as water jugs and ashtrays.

Importers and wholesalers began to compete with manufacturers and the general shop was left with little of its own but its name and reputation for personal service.

GENOZO. Ceramic, blue glaze. Ashtead Pottery. Designed by Percy Metcalf (designer of Wembley Exhibition Lion). Late 1920's. (19 cms high) .... (F)
Below - POLYCROL. Ceramic with blue glaze and black lettering. 1960's. (approx. 11 cms high) ...... (B)

FIGURES

In 1886, Thomas Barratt took Millais' 'Bubbles' and transformed it into commercial art, spending up to £126,000 p.a. on Pears' diverse and enduring advertising campaigns.

Right - Hand painted parian ware. c.1910. (14 cms high) .... (E)

Below - Painted plaster (Rocksyn). c.1930. (37 cms high) .... (F)

FIGURES

Left - ELIZABETH ARDEN. Painted plaster. c.1950. (30 cms high) ....(E)
Right - LANCÔME. White moulded rubber composition. c.1950. (30 cms high) ....(E)

Left - YARDLEY'S. Ceramic. Dresden. Early C20th. (14 cms high) ....(H. £250)
(Similar figure by Doulton, 1924, £500+. Rubber moulded version, c.1935. (E))
Right - PHOSFERINE. Painted, cast metal. c.1925. (38 cms high) ....(G)

FIGURES

Left - FREED'S. Gold coloured cast metal. c.1930. (22 cms high) ...... (F)
Middle - ALPHA NIPPER WEAR. Moulded rubber composition. c.1930. (25 cms high) ...... (E)
Right - Product unknown. Moulded rubber composition. c.1949. (48 cms high) ...... (E)

The nineteenth century, carved wooden, tobacconist Indians and Scotsmen (a relic of the time when Jacobites dominated the trade) were the precursors of the army of figures produced when trade symbols were moved from the congested street to the by then larger, better lit shop window. Enduring figural trademark models such as Johnnie Walker were accompanied by other more ephemeral creations made specifically for advertising campaigns.

Having protection from the elements, figures carved in wood could be replaced by materials more suited to mass production such as plaster, pottery, papier mâché or metal. Then, from the 1930's to the late 1950's, rubber casting became the most popular, only to be superseded by cheaper varieties of plastic.

With few exceptions, the changing styles of the twentieth century, such as Art Nouveau or Art Deco, have not impinged on the modelling of advertising figures, whose charm is more centred on their origins and the innocence of folk art. Subject matter is also uncontraversial, often whimsical and sentimental. Only historical figures or national stereotypes dare to compete with animals and children. Most figures are less than a metre high and the production run of a particular figure was usually small. Black and white dogs are ubiquitus, but only two thousand of the Morland artist were produced and Freed's ballerina was never in the corps de ballet.

FIGURES

HARDIA. Hand painted ceramic. c.1930's. (32 cms high) ....(G

FIGURES

Left - LEMON HART RUM. Moulded rubber composition. (Curzon Enterprises.) c.1930's. (25 cms high) ....(E)
Right - JOHNNIE WALKER. Moulded rubber composition. 1930-1960. (27 cms high) ....(E)
(Also found in metal, ceramic, plastic and gesso coated papier-mâché. The logo, designed in 1908, is a likeness of the firm's founder.)

Left - DEWAR'S. Moulded rubber. 1935-1960. (15 cms high) ....(D)
Middle - CLAYMORE. Ceramic. Late C19th. (31 cms high) ....(G)
Right - KING GEORGE IV. Moulded rubber. c.1950. (37 cms high) ....(E)

FIGURES

Left - PRINCE CHARLIE. Painted cast rubber. c.1950. (37 cms high) .... (E)
Right - HIGHLAND QUEEN. Bronze colour painted cast rubber. c.1950. (25 cms high) .... (E)

Left - WHITE HORSE. Plastc. Post 1960. (24 cms high) .... (C)
Right - MARTELL. Ceramic and plastic. c.1955. (24 cms high) ....(E)

FIGURES

BULMER'S. Moulded rubber composition. Pre 1955. (21 cms high)...(D)

ELY. Painted plaster. c. 1930. (29 cms high)........(F)

FLOWERS. Moulded rubber composition. Pre 1950. (25 cms high)..(E)

COURAGE. Gilded cast metal. c.1935. (31 cms high)..(E)

FIGURES

Left - Lovibond's YEOMAN ALE. Painted papier mâché. c.1925. (50 cms high) .... (F)
Middle - MARSTON'S. Ceramic. c.1960. (approx. 14 cms high) .... (D)
Right - CHARRINGTON. Painted plaster. 1930's. (24 cms high) .... (E)

Left - McEWAN'S. Moulded rubber. 1950/60. (25 cms high) .... (D)
Middle - BREWMASTER. Ceramic. Carlton Ware. Early 1960's. (24 cms high) .... (E)
Right - BARCLAY'S. Painted gesso on papier-mâché. c.1910. (65 cms high) .... (G)

FIGURES

A selection of GUINNESS'S graphic menagerie.

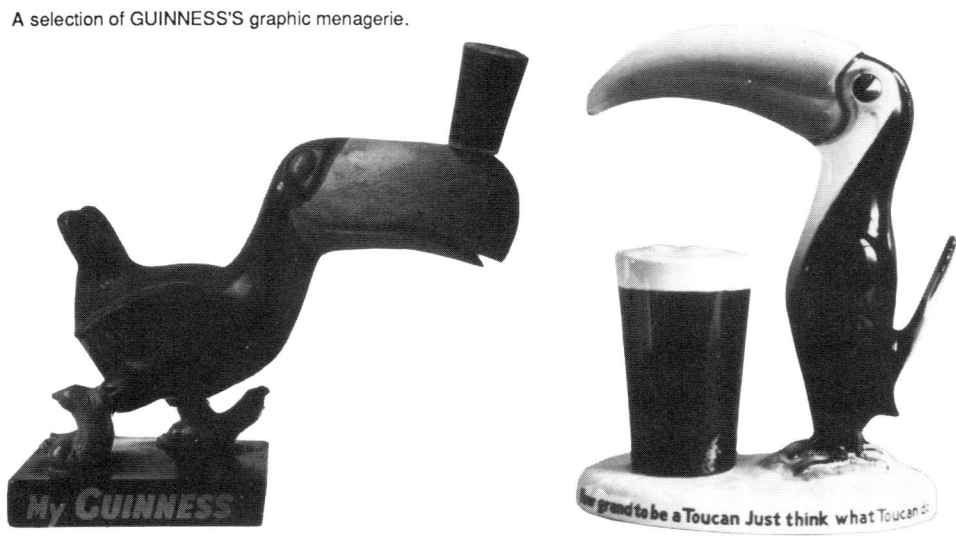

Above. Left - Soft moulded rubber. 1960's. (17 cms high) .... (D)
Right - Ceramic. Carlton Ware. 1960's. (9 cms high) .... (E)

Below. Left - Latex rubber. 1960's. (17 cms high) .... (D)
Right - Ceramic. Made in Czechoslovakia. c. 1910. (15 cms high) .... (G)
(Similar Royal Doulton example £600+.)

FIGURES

ARMY CLUB. Ceramic. Royal Doulton. 1921. (27 cms high) ....(G)

Photograph courtesy of Sothebys, Chester.

RIZLA. Coloured Terracotta. Early C20th. (84 cms high) ....(H)

WILLS. Painted plaster. 1931. (33 cms high) ....(G)

FIGURES

Right - DULUX. Ceramic. Beswick Pottery. 1964. (32 cms high) ....(H)
(As part of the Doulton group of companies Beswick pottery has recently attracted more attention and commanded higher prices.)

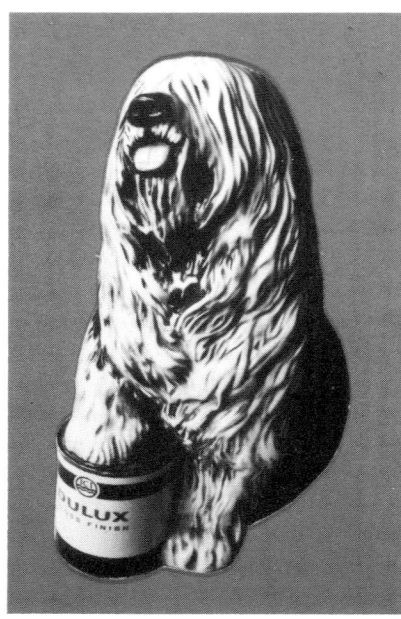

FRY'S. "Hello Daddy. Guess What I've Got." Silver plated cast metal. 1911. (18 cms high) .... (F)

NORTH BRITISH. Painted plaster. 1930's. (34 cms high) ....(F)

LIGHTS

MORLAND. Ceramic. 1950's. (25 cms high)...........(F)

GUINNESS. Ceramic (Carlton Ware) with spun aluminium revolving shade. c. 1960. (23 cms high excluding shade) ....(G)

Left - GORDON'S. Green colour pressed glass (also produced in clear glass). 1930's. (approx. 12 cms high) .....(C)
Right - GUINNESS. Plastic. c. 1955. (approx. 45 cms high) ....(D)

SHOWCARDS

DARKALINE. Multi-coloured die cut card. 1930's. (approx. 2.4 m high) .... (D)

Above - FOX'S. Free standing chromo-lithograph. Signed E. Byah. c.1925. (32 cms high) .... (D)
Below left - MILK MAID. Multi-coloured screen print. c.1955. (20 cms high) .... (B)
Below- DESBEAU. Sepia print mounted on plywood. c.1930. (28 cms high) .... (E)

SHOWCARDS

Showcards came into prominence in the 1880's when chromolithographic printing techniques had developed to a point where picture reproduction rivalled oil painting in quality.

In 1897, the Bristol company of Mardon's, one of the biggest colour printers in the country, employed some sixty in-house artists, half of whom chalked and stippled the stones for often twelve, sometimes more, colours for one showcard. As Mardon's were also specialist cardboard box manufacturers they adapted their die cutting processes to shape these cards.

Between the turn of the century and the outbreak of the First World War, the four colour lithography system and the rotary press with its metal plates began to replace traditional chromolithographic techniques and printing lost that particular associated rich texture. Companies examining their advertising strategies found retailers were not displaying all the material sent to them so advertising funds were reallocated. The showcard declined in quality and quantity to become the dull, plastic coated object of today.

RICHMOND GEM. Multi-coloured chromo-lithograph produced in two sections and slotted together. Made by Mardons (label left). Early C20th. (133 cms high) ....(£250)

SHOWCARDS

Above - STEWARD AND PATTESON'S. Multi-coloured half-tone block print. c.1930. (57 x 39 cms) (F)

Below - FRY'S. Multi-coloured chromo-lithograph. c.1900. (26.5 x 19 cms) .... (D)

Above - OGDEN'S. Multi-coloured, die cut pack display piece. c. 1935. (26 cms high) .... (D)

Below - WHITE HORSE. Five colour screen print. c.1940. (26 cms high) .... (D)

SHOWCARDS

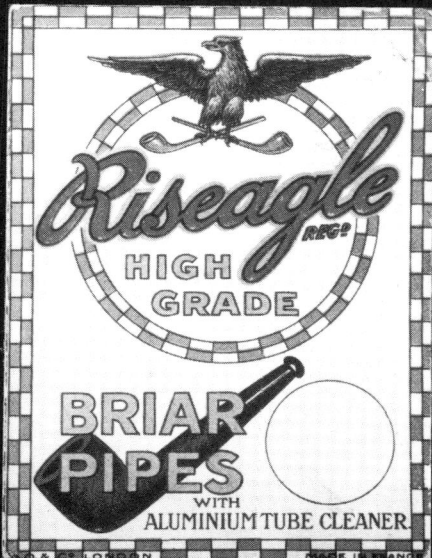

RISEAGLE. Screen printed. Silver, brown, black and blue. c.1940. (8.6 x 11.2 cms) .... (B)

SHAW SAVILL and ALBION. Multi-coloured, half tone print from a painting by Charles Dixon dated 1913. c.1928. (28 x 39 cms) .... (D)

BELL'S. Die cut, multi-coloured lithograph (designed and printed by Nathaniel Lloyd and Co.Ltd., London.) c. 1920. (42.7 cms high) .... (E)

VIMTO. Multi-coloured design by Stan Terry. c.1955. (24 x 36 cms) .... (C)

SHOWCARDS

Above - STOWER'S. Chromo-lithograph. c.1890. (23 x 30 cms - cropped) ....(D)
Below - JOHN COTTON'S. Multi-coloured. c.1935. (15.2 x 21.6 cms) ....(C)

Top - REDFORD'S. Red and black on beige card. c.1920. (approx. 22 x 9 cms) ....(B)
Above - MOON and SON. Double layered embossed die cut card. Grey and cream with applied glitter. c.1920. (34 x 39 cms) ....(D)
Below - KIWI. Multi-coloured. c. 1925. (36.8 cms high) ....(E)

SHOWCARDS

Above - PLAYER'S. Snipe shooting. Multi-coloured, plastic coated. c.1950. (25 x 20 cms) .... (C)

Right - PIRLE. Brown and blue on white. c. 1910. (19.3 x 12.7 cms) .... (C)

Bottom right - REDGATE. Multi-coloured. 1948. (37 x 24 cms) .... (C)

Below - DANDY SHANDY. Multi-coloured. c.1920. (31 x 23 cms) .... (D)

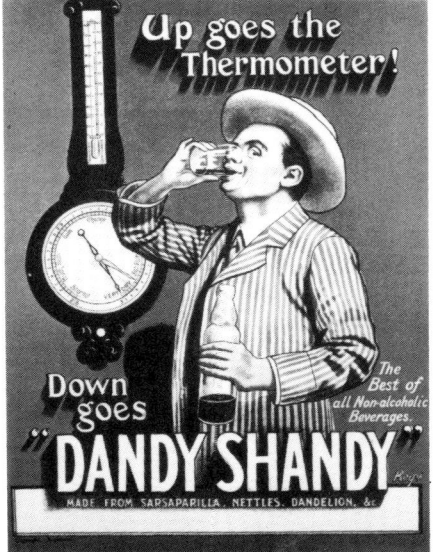

43

TIN SIGNS

Above - CUNARD. Multi-coloured transfer printed. 1920's. (24 x 20 cms) ....(G)

Below - CHAMPION. Multi-coloured transfer printed. 1930's. This sign was often used as a finger plate although not specifically designed as such. (16.5 x 6 cms) ....(D)

The history of the development of printed tin signs is not well documented. Few have a maker's mark and there is no evidence of a prominent specialist in the field. However, as production techniques were identical to those employed in the manufacture of tin boxes, key dates and possibly manufacturers were the same. A painting in the Museum of London, 'Behind the Bar', by John Henry Henshall, showing an oval Bass sign (similar to the one illustrated), dated 1882, provides evidence of concurrent use of techniques.

Unlike the more robust enamels, tin signs were almost exclusively produced for display at the point of sale. Unsuitable for exposed or damp conditions, yet more durable than paper, tin plate could be printed with fine detail which warranted close inspection.

Whether or not they were produced in large numbers, few signs in good condition have survived. Adaptations such as shelf edgings and finger plates have probably fared better, retained for their function rather than their message.

TIN SIGNS

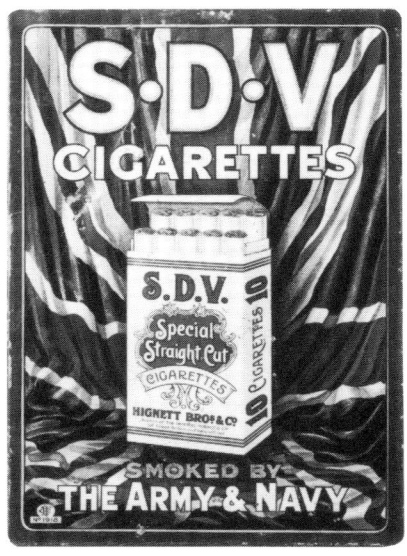

Above left - SOBRANIE. Black and white sign incorporating a container lid. c.1930. (approx. 30 cms high) ..... (E)

Above right - SDV. Multi-coloured chromo-lithograph coated with copal varnish. c.1910. (14.5 x 20.5 cms) ..... (E)

Below - TYPHOO. Embossed, yellow and black shelf sign. c. 1930. (31 cms long) .... (C)

INVINCIBLE. Multi-coloured. 1938. (53 cms wide) .... (E)

TIN SIGNS

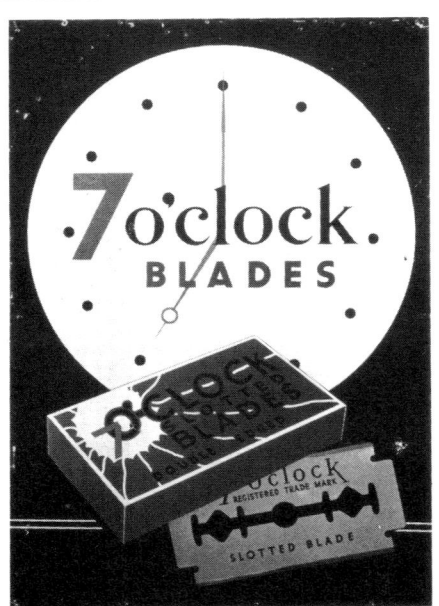

7 O'CLOCK BLADES. Cream, green, brown, red and grey printing on polished tin. c. 1935. (34.5 x 49.5 cms) .... (D)

SCHWEPPES. Multi-coloured, classic example of Art Nouveau design. c.1910. (23 x 30 cms) .... (F)

FLOR DE BELAR. Pressed tin with simulated timber frame. Multi-coloured. c.1925. (25 x 19 cms) ...... (C)

BASS. Multi-coloured, heavy duty tin with pressed frame. c.1880. (94 cms high) .... (G)

CORK. Multi-coloured, pressed frame. c.1910. (42 x 31.5 cms) .... (E)

TIN SIGNS

Above left and right - CADBURY'S. White, grey, yellow, purple and black, double sided sign. c. 1960. (13 x 37 cms) .... (D)

Above centre - HILL, EVANS & CO. Red, black, yellow and gold with shaped edge. c. 1925. (29.5 cms high) .... (E)

Below - WILSON'S. Red, black, white and gold, shaped tin label. c. 1930. (11.5 cms high) .... (B)

Above right - REDGATE. Multi-coloured. 1949. (48 x 69 cms) .... (D)
Below - CARR'S. Black, blue and yellow shelf sign. c. 1925. (35 x 1.5 cms) .... (C)

TIN SIGNS

MORELAND. Red, green, blue, black and cream, embossed tin. c.1928. (56 x 56 cms)......................(F)

STAFF ALLENS. Multi-coloured, painted tin on wood. 1935. (30.5 cms diameter).......................................(E)

SIFTA. Two tone blue, red and white, transfer printed alloy. c.1950. (19 x 24 cms)........................(D)

MILLER. Black, red and white, cut out, double sided sign on wooden stand. c.1935. (40.5 cms high)......(E)

BORAX. Red, black and cream. 1925. (61 x 18 cms) ....(C)

MELOX. Multi-coloured chromo-lithographic print on embossed tin. c.1920 (49.5 x 34.2 cms)................(E)

DISPENSERS

BONZA. Red, blue, black and white tin. c.1930. (16 cms diameter) ....(C)

Right - ALONO. Red, white, brown and green, string tin with cutter. (17.5 cms overall height) ....(D)

String, hot water and net curtain wire are far from glamorous commodities yet well packaged they become attractive, even exciting. The more exotic or dramatic the display unit or dispenser the more memorable: a castle turret for hot water or an extraordinary golden slipper to take a nylon sheathed leg.

Manufacturers commissioned and supplied shop fittings embellished with their logos for shopkeepers to buy at discount prices with the optimistic proviso that they be used solely for display of that company's goods. Many cabinets and cases have outlived their contractual obligations and joined the annoying list of items in antique shops, not for sale.

RIGHT - BOVRIL. Copper plated, metal urn with brass accessories. c.1900. (43 cms high) ....(G)

DISPLAY PIECES

Above - SYLKO. Cream, blue, red and gold, paper coated, wooden chest of drawers. c.1950. (35 x 22 x 14 cms) .... (D)

Above left - MacNIVEN and CAMERON. Dark stained pine with gilded lettering behind glass, pen display case. c.1920. (35.5 cms wide) .... (E)

Left - BALLITO. Black and gold, fibre plaster and wood, hosiery display stand. c.1935. (16 cms high) .... (C)

Below-PARKER. Multi-coloured card cut out. c.1945. (28.5 cms diameter) .... (D)

Below - ST. IVEL. Parian ware impressed, "Made in Thuringia for Aplin and Barrett." c. 1900. (16 cms high) .... (F)

CONDIMENT POTS

A collection of small scale Doulton ceramic containers for mustard, salt and pepper.
Top - Two tone brown with white sprigging. Early C20th. ....(D)
Centre - Blue, green and ochre glaze with incised decoration. c.1895. .... (E)
Bottom - Two tone brown with brown transfer printed lettering. Early C20th. ....(D)

ASHTRAYS

Top left - FORREST. Black and white, Grafton China. c 1920. (9 cms diameter)..(C

Above - GREENE KING. Green and blue glazed, Roya Doulton pottery. c.1910. (12 cms diameter)......(D

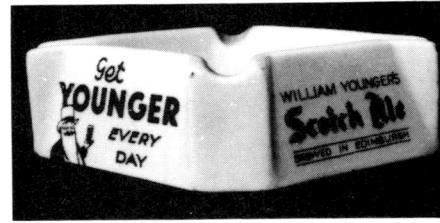

BRASSO. Brass. c.1930. (10 cms diameter).........(C)

YOUNGER'S. Black transfer on white, Royal Doulto pottery. 1937. (9 cms square)................................(C

Below - TIMPSON FINE SHOES. Green glaze with hand painted, multi-coloured figure. Beswick Pottery. c.1965. (17 cms diameter).......................................(D)

Below - TWYFORDS. Black transfer on white pottery Rare. c.1945. (14.5 cms maximum width)..............(D

MATCHBOX STANDS

Above - M. B. FOSTER. Blue and green glazed stoneware marked Doulton, Lambeth. c.1890's. (13 cms diameter) ....(D)

At the turn of the century when smoking was acceptable in the convivial atmosphere of pubs and cafés free matches were provided in strikers and stands. Matchbooks later put advertising in the customer's pocket and the displays of individual matches finally disappeared with the austerity of World War Two.

Right - WATSON'S. Honey glaze over a black, pictorial transfer. c.1925. (13.5 cms maximum width) (D)

Below right - WORTHINGTON. Red and black transfer on white ceramic with metal bell. c.1925. (approximately 11 cms high) ....(D)

Below left - BRYANT and MAY. Cast metal. c. 1890. (10.5 cms high) ....(D)

BASS. Green and red transfer on white ceramic. c.1930's. (6 cms high) ....(C)

53

MATCH STRIKERS

HAIG. Black transfer on cream ceramic. R. Hammersley and Son, Burslem. Pre 1905. (5 cms high) .... (D)

DEWAR'S. Honey and green glazed ceramic with sprigged lettering. Royal Doulton. c.1910. (14.5 cm diameter) .... (E)

DANIELLS. Black transfer on two tone brown ceramic. c.1925. (approx. 10 cms high) .... (F)

Below - DUNVILLE'S. Black and red transfer on cream ceramic. Shelley Late Foley. Late 1920's. (12 cms diameter) .... (D)

MUMBY'S. Two tone blue ceramic with raised white letters. c.1920. (5.4 cms high) .... (E)

FRAINS. Two tone green ceramic with white sprig and black impressed letters. Lovatt Langley Mill c.1910. (8 cms high) .... (D)

MATCH STRIKERS

Right - STONE'S. Black transfer on cream ceramic. 'Proprietors The Finsbury Distillery Co.' on base. c.1930. (10 cms diameter) .... (D)

Below - BARRETT. Two tone brown ceramic with black transfer c.1920. (approx. 12 cms high) .... (F)

DON BREWERY. Black transfer on white ceramic. c.1910. (approx. 7 cms high) .... (E)

Below - OLD BUSHMILLS. Black and orange transfer and coloured enamel painting on cream ceramic. Impressed 'Fielding' on base. c.1920. (8 cms diameter) .... (D)

BUCKNALL. Black transfer and enamel colouring on white ceramic. c.1920. (approx. 10 cms high) .... (E)

TRAYS

LEWIS'S. Black transfer with maroon lining on white ceramic. c.1910. (16 cms diameter) .... (D)

HIGHLAND QUEEN. Multi-coloured, transfer printed tin. c.1960. (31.7 cms diameter) .... (B)

These utilitarian items have been use for promotional advertising since the mid 1880's. Grocers, butchers and bakers had ceramic trays for unpackaged goods while publicans employed more robust enamelled metal or brass. Impressed bakelite found favour in the 1930's but screen printed metal versions were more colourful and remain popular. Advertising trays are still produced by drinks companies but like fresh sawdust have all but disappeared from shops. Unimaginatively, fast food establishments only supply plain plastic with stuck on paper inserts.

Left - BALLOON. Black transfer on white ceramic. c.1910. (38.5 x 31.5 cms) Rare .... (F)
Below - ANDREW AND ATKINSON'S. White, blue and red enamel. c.1930. (30 cms diameter) .... (D)

COASTERS

Above - A fine collection of brewery coasters made between 1890 and 1930. 10 cms, 13 cms or 16 cms diameter.
JACOBS, FLOWERS, BASS .... (D) both WORTHINGTONS .... (E)
YOUNGERS, both ALLSOPP'S, BARCLAY, CANNON .... (F)

COASTERS

Humble in function, these elaborately decorated ceramic coasters or jug stands have the decorative style of Gothic revival eclecticism used in the interior design of prestigious Victorian city pubs. Occasionally to be found with silver mounts they blended with the etched glass screens, mahogany panelling, polished brass and Corinthian columns which met florid plaster moulding on high fretted ceilings.

Most surviving coasters were produced by Copeland and some are marked Cauldon or Minton. They are rare and minor damage seems acceptable to the small band of dedicated collectors.

Four of the most desirable beer coasters, all from the nineteenth century, in very fine condition. .... (F)

MEASURES

Two tone blue transfer on white ceramic. c. 1850. (12.5 cms high) .... (E)

BIGG'S. Black transfer on white ceramic with an early bluish colour clear glaze. c.1850. (10 cms high) Rare. .... (F)

J. TAMS. Black transfer on white ceramic with blue and red lining and red handle decoration. VR 82 lead pint excise mark set into base. 1882 patent. (11.5 cms high). .... (E)

JACOB MORDON. Salt glazed with dipped top. Staffordshire excise mark. Incised 1750. Extremely rare. .... (£500+)

Advertising collectables, Victorian tiles, stripped pine, Bauhaus chairs and plants can live happily together without turning a home into a museum.

TINS

PACKAGING

Competitive, large scale production for wide distribution made branding and printed prepackaging inevitable. The shopkeeper was no longer required to blend, measure or wrap when his skills were replaced by a blossoming packaging industry which was only constrained by current technology and marketing strategies.

Above - VICTORY V. Multi-coloured with working clock. c.1910. (approx. 32 cms high) .... (E)

Above left - BLUE BOY TOFFEE. Multi-coloured. c.1930. (approx. 30 cms wide) .... (D)

Below - W. DUNMORE and SON, LTD. Gold with dark blue embossed, art nouveau style decoration and brown velvet pin cushion. c.1910. (11 x 25.5 x 6 cms) .... (E)

TINS

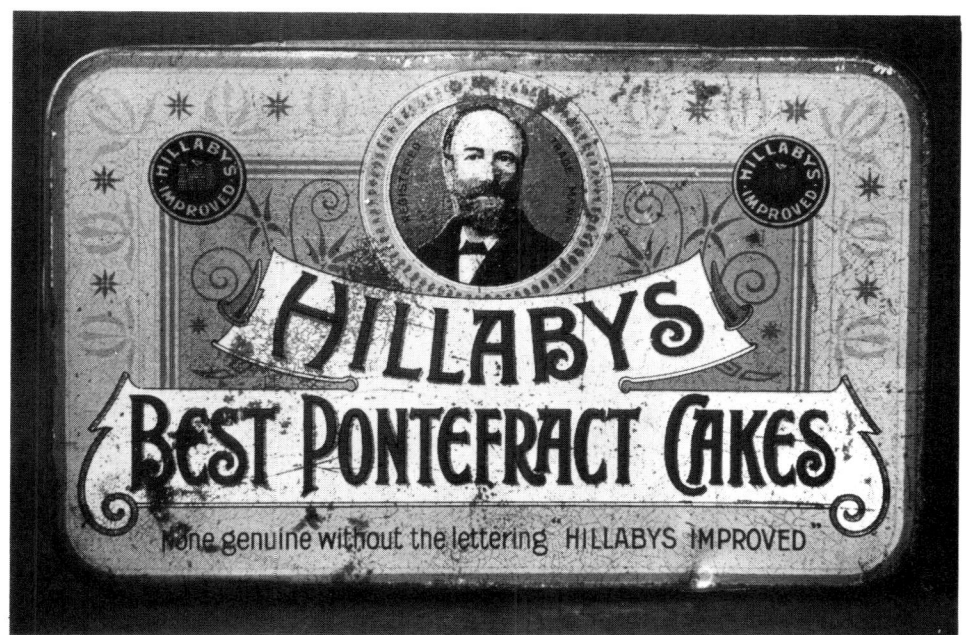

HILLABYS. Multi-coloured. Marked Hudson Scott and Sons Ltd., Carlisle. c.1912. (22 x 14 x 10 cms) ....(C)

Few late eighteenth century handpainted, tin plated tea canisters survive and early nineteenth century sealed food tins developed for military commissariats were neither reusable nor decorative. Tins with direct stencilling, paper or soldered, embossed metal labels have none of the attractive qualities of full colour printing on tin which was not developed until the mid nineteenth century.

The technique of chromolithography used to produce colour prints on paper could not easily be applied directly to non-porous, rigid tin plate and transfer paper, also used by potteries, was applied to the tin and soaked off leaving behind the ink which was then varnished.

In 1877, the metal box makers, Huntley, Boorne and Stevens, whose main clients were Huntley and Palmers, acquired the exclusive right to a new offset lithography process which avoided the use of transfer paper. When this patent elapsed in 1879 other manufacturers adopted the process and a period of exquisite design and decoration followed lasting until the 1920's when styles and techniques changed again.

Reports of the use to which empty tins were put encouraged some manufacturers to exploit the tin box's potential as an ornament, child's toy and useful container. Logos were more discretely placed and figural shapes produced, a tradition revitalised by the gift shop tins designed for the collector's market today.

TINS

A small collection of miniature tins, all under 115 mm longest dimension. PUNCH and JUDY and FOOTBALL. Unnamed. .... (C)   GRANDFATHER CLOCK. Rowntrees. c. 1925. ....(E)   HUNTLEY and PALMERS. Above. c. 1950. ....(E)   Below. c. 1932. ....(D)   BUTTERFLIES. Rowntrees. c. 1920. ....(D) EPPS'S. c. 1900. ....(E)   CRICKET BAT. Rowntrees. c. 1920. ....(D)

TINS

Above - RED INDIAN GERM. Yellow, red, white and brown. c.1938. (5 cms diameter) .... (B)

Above right - SULPHUR. Ochre and brown. 1930's. (5.5 cms diameter) .... (A)

Right - BORACIC. Cream, pink, red, black, green and gold. c.1930. (5 cms diameter) .... (A)

Below right - MATTHEWS'. White, green, red and black. 1950's. (7 cms diameter) .... (A)

Below - EMARCO. Two tone blue. 1930's. (6 cms diameter) .... (A)

TINS

Above left - C.W.S. sample tin. Red, green, yellow, black and gold. c.1900. (5.2 cms high) ....(D)
Above right - TABLOID TEA. Multi-coloured sample tin. 1880's. (8 cms wide) ....(D)

As at the start of their development, tins are still used for packaging fine tea and tobacco but many have been replaced by plastic containers and, sadly, those exquisite, miniature free sample tins seem to have disappeared forever.

Below - MAZAWATTEE - Multi-coloured. Marked 3/- one pound. Designed, decorated and manufactured at the Mazawattee Works, New Cross. c.1910. (18 x 16 x 6.5 cms) ....(D)

TINS

Above left - MAZAWATTEE. Multi-coloured sample tin. c.1885. (5.5 cms high) ....(D)
Above centre - EPPS'S. Multi-coloured sample tin with different pictures on each face. c.1890. (5 cms high) ......(D)
Above right - LUTONA. Multi-coloured, dual purpose, sample tin. c.1890. (5 cms high) ....(D)
Below left - CALEDONIA. Multi-coloured. c. 1920. (approx. 21 cms in diameter) ....(C)
Below right - DR THOMPSON. Multi-coloured, screw top. c. 1925. (18 cms high) ....(D)

COLMAN'S. Mustard Manufacturers to the Queen. Multi-coloured. c.1900. (14 x 20 x 14 cms) ....(D)

TINS

C.W.S. Crumpsall Biscuits. Multi-coloured. c.1900. (26 x 11 x 6 cms) ....(D)

Above - L N E R 'ENGINE' by MacFarlane, Lang & Co. Green, silver, white and black. 1937. (35 cms long) ......(H)
Below - 'Coronation Coach' by W & R Jacob. Multi-coloured. (Originally boxed.) 1936. (23 cms long) ....(G)

TINS

CARR & CO. Biscuit Manufacturers of Carlisle. A multi-coloured, typical 1890's tin probably produced by the Hudson Scott Company of Carlisle. (12 x 6 x 9 cms) ....(E)

TINS

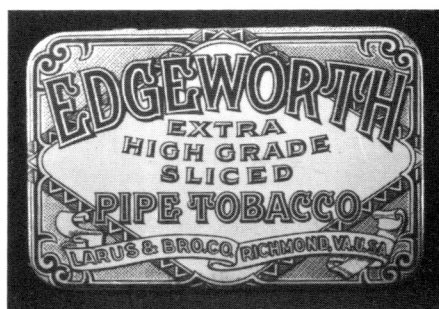

Top left - SQUADRON LEADER. Multi-coloured. c.1935. (11 cms wide) ......(C)
Top right - SAM'S OWN. Ochre, brown and black. c.1930. (11 cms wide) ......(C)
Above left - PLAYER'S AIRMAN. Multi-coloured. c.1930. (10 cms wide) ......(C)
Above right - EDGEWORTH. Two tone blue and silver. c.1945. (8 cms wide) ......(B)
Below - HIGNETT'S. Multi-coloured. A classic Edwardian tin. (14.5 cms wide) ......(E)

TINS

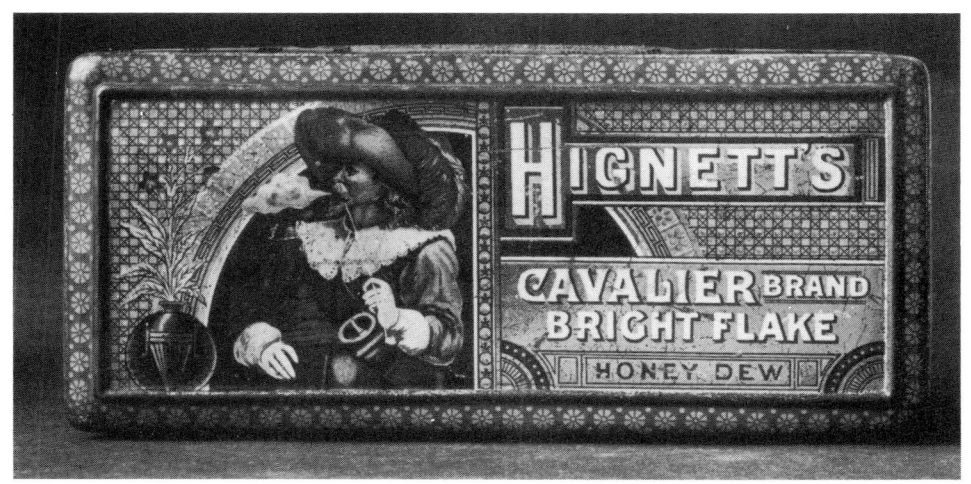

Above - HIGNETT'S. Multi-coloured. c. 1912. (18 cms wide) ....(F)
(Hignett was one of thirteen companies who amalgamated in 1901 to form the Imperial Tobacco Company.)

Below left - SALMON & GLUCKSTEIN'S. Yellow, black, gold and red. c.1910. (10.5 cms wide) ....(D)

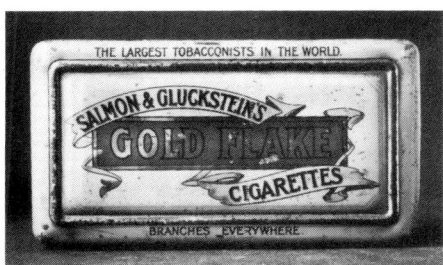

RATTLER. Multi-coloured. c. 1915. (17 cms wide) ....(E)

SIR WALTER RALEIGH. White, black and orange. Flip top lid. c.1935. (11 cms high) ....(C)

TINS

MURRAY'S. Yellow and red. c. 1945. (11 cms wide) .... (B)

OGDEN'S. Red, white, blue and brown. c. 1930. (11 cms wide) .... (B)

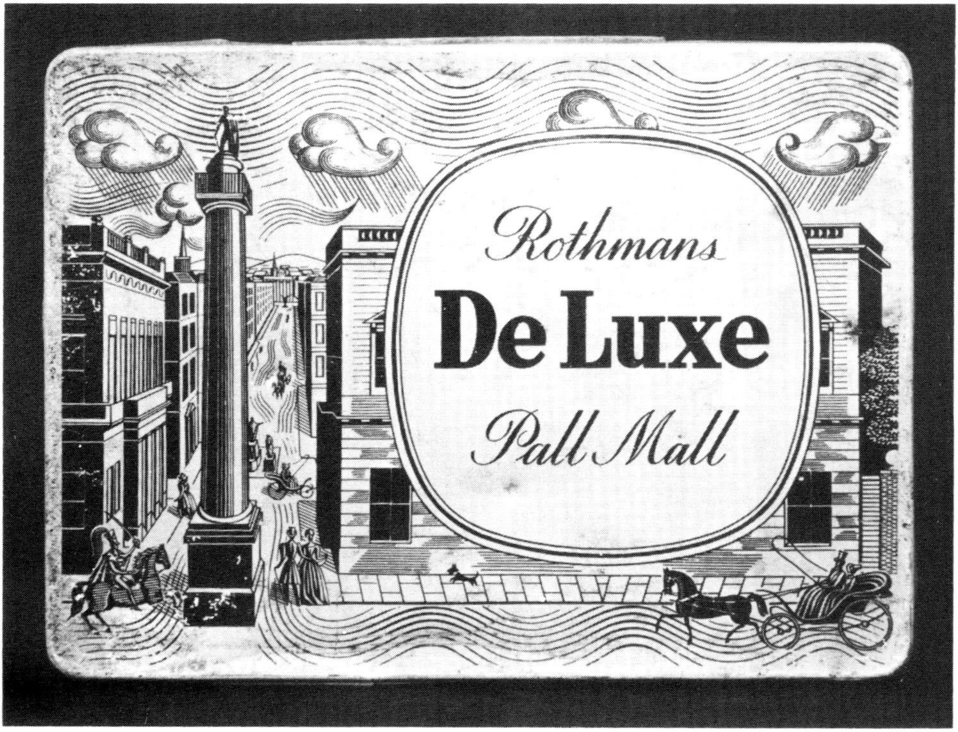

ROTHMANS. Black, white and grey. A future classic tin designed by the Radio Times illustrator, Eric Frazer. c.1951. (15 cms wide) ....(C)

TINS

AFRIKANDER. Red, yellow, cream and brown, curved pocket tin. c.1930. (8.5 cms wide) .... (D)

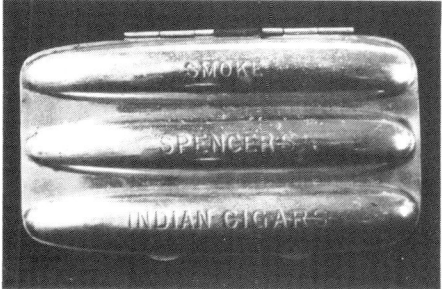

SPENCER'S. An unusual aluminium cigar package. 1930's. (13 cms long) .... (C)

MacDONALD'S. Multi-coloured. c.1900. (8 cms high) ....(D)

LAMBERT & BUTLER'S. Gold, pale blue, black, green and red, embossed design. 1930's. (13 cms wide) .... (C)

MORRIS. Yellow, red, black and gold. c.1910. (10.5 cms wide). Rare. .... (C)

TINS

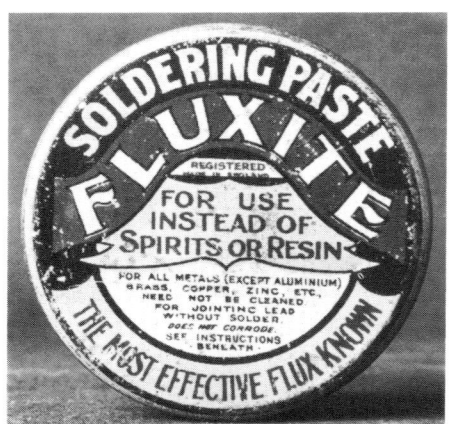

Above - FLUXITE. Pink, cream, black and green. c.1938. Representative of a rather neglected area of collecting. (5 cms diameter) .... (A)

Below right - HALFORDS. Green, black and white. 1960's. (19 cms high) .... (C)

Below - CURTIS'S and HARVEY'S. Red, blue and pale green on cream. c.1920. A rare paper label. (16.5 cms high) .... (D)

FRONTIER. Multi-coloured, rare pictorial. c.1910. (4.5 cms diameter) .... (D)

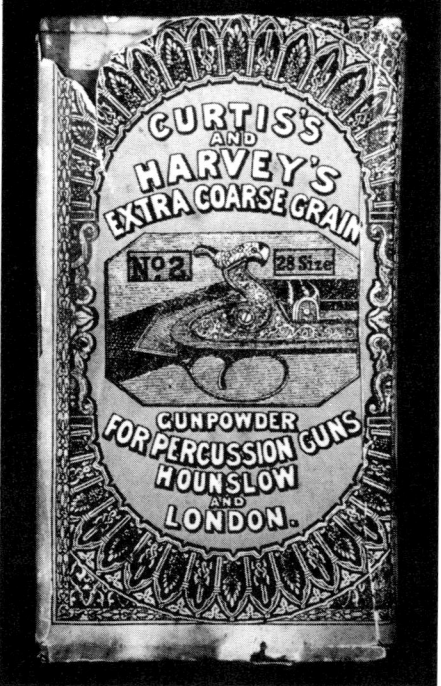

VESTAS

Above - J. N. MASTERS. Gold colour metal. Inscribed VR 1837 - 1901 on reverse. (5 cms wide) .... (D)

Centre right - BOURNVILLE. Red, black and orange with gilt edge. c. 1920. (6.5 cms wide) .... (D)

Below - MAZAWATTEE. Sepia and brown, Louis Wain design. Striker back. c.1920. (6 cms high) .... (E)

IMPERIAL HOTEL. Cream and black label on gilt box impressed Bryant and May's wax vestas on the back. c.1920. (4.5 cms wide) .... (D)

Below - HMV. Aluminium needle tin with striker back. c.1935. (5.25 cms wide) .... (C)

Below - BRYANT and MAY. Plated tin. c.1890. (4.5 cms wide) .... (D)

MATCHBOXES

In 1827, John Walker, a chemist in Stockton-on-Tees, sold his unpatented friction match in a tin box of 100 for 1s 2d. Soon 'lucifers', 'congreves' or 'fuzees' were widely available and in 1861 the partnership of Bryant and May, erstwhile importers and distributors of Swedish matches, opened their own London patent safety match factory. Their opinion that elaborate, expensive labels would guard against imitation and be cheap in the long run helped to stimulate an amazing range of matchbox label designs which have intrigued phillumenists ever since.

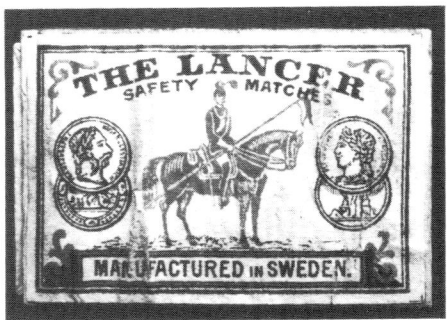

Above - THE LANCER. Red and black on beige paper label. c.1910. (5.3 cms wide).........................(B)

Above left - THE AUTOMOBILE. Red and black on beige paper label. c.1910. (5.3 cms wide).............(B)

Centre left - ROYAL MATCHES. Blue, yellow, red, black and pink printing. c.1912. (5.3 cms wide).......(B)

THE LOCOMOTIVE. Red and black on beige paper. c.1910. (5.8 cms wide)..(B)

HARLEQUIN. Black, red, green and yellow. c. 1930. (5.5 cms high) ....(C)

BOXES

Not designed for secondary usage, cardboard boxes are normally kept only until their contents have gone. Although old toys are more prized if complete with their original box, the attractions of other graphically decorated boxes have yet to be appreciated.

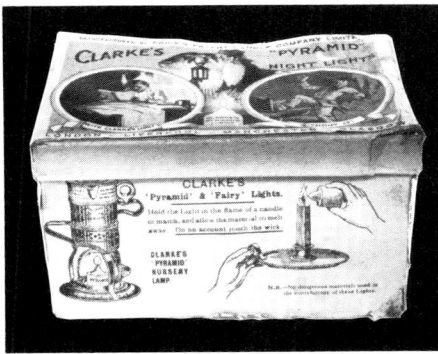

Top - WIGTOWNSHIRE CREAMERY. Beige with dark blue printing. c. 1910. (33 cms wide) ....(D)

Centre - CLARKE'S. Multi-coloured wrap around label and black printing directly on box. c. 1930. (13 cms wide) ....(B)

Right - WRIGHT'S. Two tone blue and yellow. 1930's or 1950's. (17.5 cms high) ....(C)

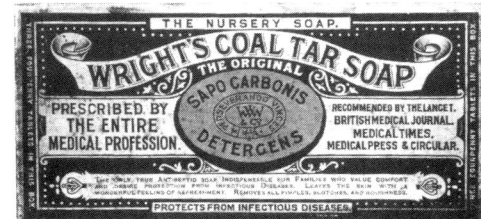

Left - LYONS'. Gold, two tone blue, red and black. c.1930. (25 cms wide) ....(C)
Right - WRIGHT'S. Brown and yellow on white. c.1920. (17.5 cms wide) ....(C)

77

PACKETS

Below - LIBRARY. Multi-coloured chromo-lithograph. c.1920. (12 x 7 cms) .... (B)

Above - ARMY AND NAVY. Multi-coloured. c.1920. (12 x 6.5 cms) .... (B)

Below - FLORA MacDONALD. Gold and black on pale blue. c.1930. (5 x 3.5 cms) .... (A)

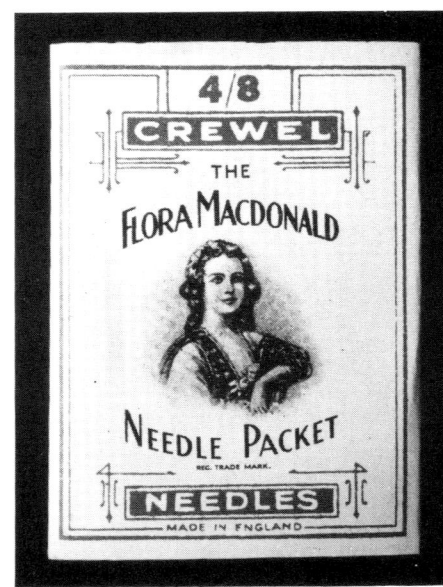

Below - COMPLETE. White on blue. c. 1925. (14.5 x 9 cms) .... (A)

Above - RELIABLE. Gold and red on white. c. 1930. (7 x 3 cms) .... (A)

Above - HENRY MILWARD. Black on blue. c.1935. (5 x 2.5 cms) .... (A)

PACKETS

Above left - DOUBLE ACE. Red, white and black. c. 1925. (6.8 x 4 cms) ....(B)

Above centre - BIG BEN. Red, white, blue and brown. c. 1948. (4.5 x 2.5 cms) ....(A)

Above right - HIGNETT'S. Pink, red, black and gold on white. Dummy packet. c. 1910. (7.5 x 4.5 cms) (C)

Right - PLAYER'S dummy packets. Foil and gold, red, white and blue paper labels. c.1930. (5 x 4.5 x 2.5 cms) ....(B)

Below left - IVY. Green and sepia on white. c. 1945. (11.5 x 9.5 cms) ....(A)
Below right - LONDON. Gold, black, white and green. c.1935. (8.5 x 5 cms) ....(A)

WRAPPING PAPER

Fine decorative papers for skilled grocers to pack and wrap dry goods such as tea and coffee. (White sugar was normally packed in the thicker 'sugar' paper.) .... VASEY'S (D) others (C)

LABELS

Top line, left to right - 1900/10, 1920's, c.1900. Centre line - Mid 1930's. Bottom line, left to right - 1950's, 1910, 1940's. Individual value ....(A)
As with cigarette cards, framed and mounted collections of labels have great decorative appeal.

MILK BOTTLE TOPS

Simply printed in one or two colours, these waxed card discs are mostly collected by dairy enthusiasts. .... (A)

Although milk has been bottled for over a hundred years it was only after the First World War that the use of milk bottles became widespread and the less hygienic practice of ladling from churn to jug began to disappear. Unlegislated standardisation is rare and the wide necked bottle generally adopted by hundreds of small dairies in the 1920's must be a design classic.

The waxed cardboard disc seals used then generally simply identified the product but were sometimes printed with a dairy company name or advertised something used with milk. The bottles are found embossed or screen printed by 'ACE' (Applied Colour Enamel) with

MILK BOTTLES

company names sometimes embellished with cows or yoked milkmaids and they also carried brand advertising which even allowed the association of milk with cigarette smoking.

By the mid 1950's, hygiene regulations had disposed of the cardboard disc, depriving both schoolboys and woolly pompom makers of its secondary uses. Now, milkmen, the last of the domestic delivery men, are declining in number as supermarket cartons win popularity from the bottle.

Above, left to right - EXPRESS. Double-sided. Late 1950's. ....(C) GREEN'S. c.1975. Very few produced therefore price by negotiation. OVALTINE. (Rockwell bottle.) Double-sided, 'Player's Please' on reverse. 1930's. ....(D)

Right - ACE. Durable labels. Display bottle. c. 1937. ....(D)

Below, left to right - PRICE. Late 1930's. ...(C) SMITH. 1940's. ....(B) PLAYER'S. 'Ovaltine' on reverse. 1930's. ....(D)

BOTTLES

In the nineteenth century packaging boom glass and pottery producers competed with each other, developing new techniques to meet the growing demand. Glass making benefited from a series of patent mould designs which allowed more variation in shape and embossing but although moulds were used for clay, most commercial pottery was still hand thrown as an efficient potter could produce twelve hundred bottles a day. However, time consuming drying, glazing and firing processes could not be eliminated from pottery production and by the time fully automated glass bottle making machines came into use in the 1920's orders for ceramic containers had slumped and never recovered.

Although the attractiveness of dark blue glass seems to be universally appreciated, for most serious bottle collectors there is a c.1925 dateline when hand finished (applied lip, burst or sheared top) bottles were supersede by the more bland machine made variety; and it is only recently that collectors have sought items complete with their original labels.

Above - Cobalt blue glass with black on white printed label. c.1925. (13.3 cms high) .... (C)

Illustrated below, a small sample of the more common poison variants .... (B - D)

BOTTLES

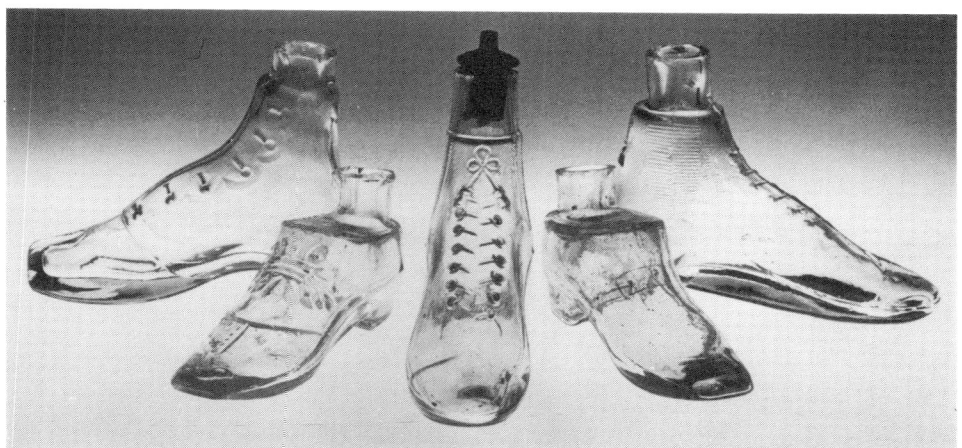

Above - Aqua glass, perfume or cologne. c.1900. (5 - 8 cms high) ....(D)

Bottle guides and directories usually catalogue bottles according to contents although many collections have other themes such as place of origin, colour or shape. It is not always easy to determine the original contents of most figural bottles which were produced for inks, perfumes, sweets and spirits as many were unmarked excepted for paper labels. Unlabelled bottles retrieved from Victorian rubbish dumps have been enjoyed for their hand finished, imperfect individuality and tactile qualities but growing interest in their history has stimulated a search for labelled examples.

Below - Blue, green and aqua penny perfumes. 1880 - 1900. (5 - 9.8 cms high) ...... Blue (D). Green and aqua (C)

BOTTLES

Above left - PARKER. Two tone blue, orange, black and white label. c.1935. (7.3 cms high). Ink bottles such as these are generally ignored by collectors. .... (A)
Above centre - ENDORSING INK. Clear glass bottle; black printing on white paper label. c.1935. (10 cms high) (A)
Above right - HELIOTROPE. Clear glass bottle; gold, red and white label. c.1935. (7.3 cms high). Another ignored but attractive category. .... (A)

Above - Various green, stoppered, smelling salts bottles. 1890's - 1940's. (up to 9 cms high) .... (C)

BOTTLES

The shapes and colours of bottles or jars might suggest their contents but more information was needed and although glass embossing or impressed marks on ceramics could convey quite elaborate messages these were usually subtle and sometimes difficult to read. Advances in paper making and printing techniques made printed paper labels relatively cheap and attractive and by the 1830's they were used on most forms of ceramic or glass packaging. By the 1850's chromolithographic printing gave added scope for glamorous designs which not only named the contents but could convey a company's image throughout a range of its products. However, on reusable containers paper labels would be washed off and some pottery producers adopted the technique of underglaze transfer printing to provide permanently identifiable labels.

Right - EVERGREEN AMMONIA. Black transfer on stoneware. Govancroft Pottery. c.1925. (28 cms high) Rare. .... (D)
Far right - PLYNINE AMMONIA. Black transfer on stoneware. c.1900. (27 cms high) .... (C)

Below left - COOPER. Black transfer on white body. c.1900. (13 cms high) .... (D)
Below right - LEICESTER MAGIC. Black transfer on stoneware. c.1910. (11 cms high) .... (C)

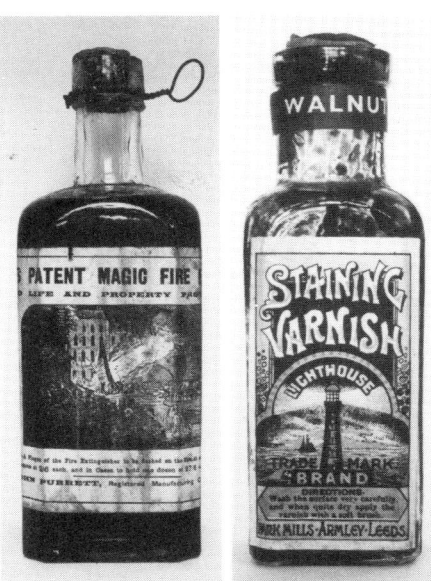

Above left - PATENT MAGIC FIRE. Black on white printed label on aqua bottle. c.1885. (23 cms high) Extremely rare. .... (G)
Above right - LIGHTHOUSE VARNISH. Two tone blue and yellow on white label. c.1930. (14 cms high) ... (C)

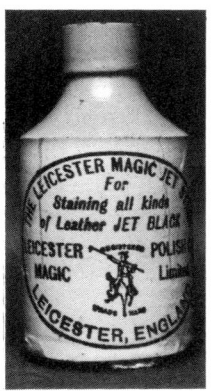

BOTTLES

Above - Various transfer printed stout bottles by Buchan, Portobello. c.1910. (All 20 cms high) ....(D)

Left - CRESSWELL. Aqua glass codd bottle, unusual size. c.1920. (25 cms tall) ....(D)

Below - 'Bristol green glaze', slabsealed stoneware. First half C19th. (All 17 cms high). Condition and clarity of seal is the main pricing variable. ....(D - F)
Generally referred to as ginger beers, there is no documentary evidence as to the contents of these bottles although their shape would indicate hop bitters, stout or mineral water.

BOTTLES

Top left - OXFORD. Embossed. Bright bottle green. c.1900. (16 cms high) ....(C)
Top centre - ROYAL GERMAN. Embossed. Dark green amber. Early flat base and applied lip. (Seltzer bottles of this general shape were produced from the 1850's or earlier, with pontilled bases.) c.1855. (13.7 cms high) ....(E)
Right - STOWER'S. Embossed. Aqua. Multi-coloured paper label and lead seal. c.1920. (36.5 cms high) ....(D)
Bottom, left to right - HAWKES. Screw stoppered, two tone, black transfer. c.1935. (16.5 cms high) ....(C)
TURNBULL. Swing stopper, two tone black transfer. c.1920. (20 cms high) ....(D)
CLAYTON'S. Two tone, brown top with crown cork seal, black rubber stamp transfer. c.1930. (18.5 cms high) ... (C)

STORAGE JARS

WRIGHT BISCUITS. Clear glass with gilded engraved lettering. c.1925. (28 cms high) .... (E)

STANDARD SWEETS. Clear glass with ground glass top. Beige, gold, blue, red and orange on white paper labels. c.1930. (47 cms high) .... (F)

OGDEN'S. Clear glass with red infilled engraved lettering. Metal lid with red lettering on black and wooden knob. c.1920. (14 cms diameter) .... (D)

STORAGE JARS

 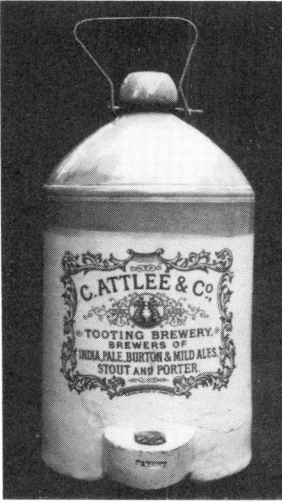 

Above, left to right - SHUCKFORD & SPEEDY. Black transfer, two tone, Fulham Pottery. c.1890. (Company taken over by Taylor Walker in 1927.) (35 cms high) ....(D)
C. ATTLEE & CO. Black transfer, two tone, Fulham Pottery. 1901-7. (33 cms high) ....(D)
C. HAMMERTON & CO. Black transfer, two tone, Fulham Pottery. c.1920. (35 cms high) ....(D)

Below, left to right - USHER'S. Black transfer, two tone, Fulham Pottery. 1890 - 1919. (27 cms high) ....(D)
WRIGHT & GREIG. Black transfer, two tone, Buchan, Portobello. c.1890. (43 cms high). Like all these flagons, an extreme rarity. ....(G)
THORNE BROS. Black transfer, two tone, Fulham Pottery. c.1890. (Company taken over by Meux's in 1914.) (35 cms high) ....(E)

POTS

Above, left to right. DEVONSHIRE CREAM. Black transfer on white. c.1900. (8.5 cms high) ....(C)
LANCASHIRE DAIRIES. Black transfer, brown top. Port Dundas Pottery. 1910. (7.5 cms high) ....(B)
BUTTERCUP CREAM. Blue transfer, blue top. c.1910. (11.5 cms high) ....(D)

Underglaze blue transfer printed pot lids were produced from the 1830's and multi-coloured Prattware from 1845 but a gap of a hundred years exists between the development of ceramic transfer techniques and their general widespread commercial use in the 1880's. The reasons for this are uncertain but the cheapness of paper labels, the labour costs of applying transfers and the lack of a sufficiently dense black ceramic ink might all have contributed. Now only small amounts of transfer printed ceramic packaging are produced, some commissioned by stores like Harrod's and Fortnum and Mason's who trade on their own traditions.

Below, left to right. BUTTERCUP butter crock. Two tone, black transfer, with lid. 5lb size. Buchan. c.1920. (17 cms high) ....(E)
MAYPOLE DAIRY. Two tone, black transfer, with handle. c.1925. (15 cms high) ....(E)

POTS

Above - Three of the most common, black transferred, white paste pots.
Left to right - SAINSBURY'S. c. 1920. (6.5 cms high) ....(A)
BURGESS'S. c.1910. (9.8 cms diameter) ....(B)
POULTON & NOEL. c.1920. (9 cms high) ....(B)

Above left - GILSON & SON'S. Royal blue transfer. c.1890. (approx. 11 cms diameter) ....(E)
Above right - BROOKES & CO. Orange brown transfer. c. 1890. (approx. 8 cms diameter) ....(E)
Below, left to right - CROSSE & BLACKWELL. Black transfer on both sides. Late C19th. (11 cms high) ....(D)
ARISTON. Blue transfer. Late 1930's. (8.8 cms high). Rare ....(C)
FRANK COOPER'S. Black transfer, miniature or sample pot. c.1910. (5.4 cms high) ....(D)

  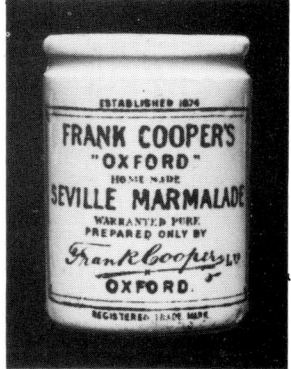

POTS

Top left - KNOWLES'. Black transfer. c.1885. (5.2 cms diameter) .... (E)
Top right - ARMY & NAVY. Black transfer on celluloid top. c.1930. (4.5 cms diameter). Rare .... (C)
Above left - SAVAGE'S. Black transfer. c. 1885. (approx. 6 cms diameter) .... (E)
Above right - KRANOL. c.1900. (approx. 8 cms diameter) .... (E)
Below - HOLLOWAY'S. Black transfer. His and her variations. Late C19th. (3.7 cms high) .... (D)

POTS

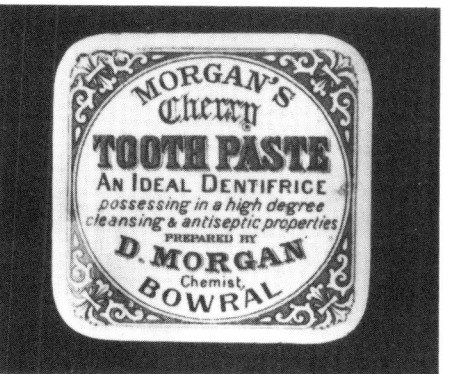

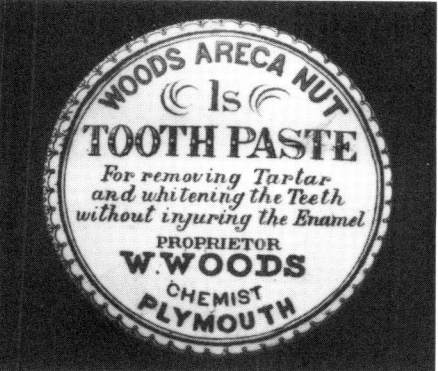
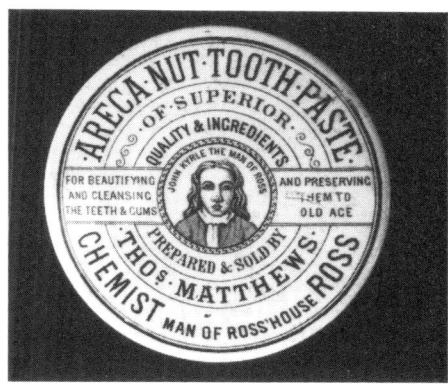

Top left - MORGAN'S. Black transfer. Very rare Australian lid found in UK. c.1900. (7 cms square) .... (F)
Top right - SAVARS. Black transfer. c.1890. (7 cms diameter) .... (C)
Above left - WOODS. Black transfer. Early C20th. (7.5 cms diameter) .... (C)
Above right - THOMAS MATTHEWS. Black transfer. c.1885. (7 cms diameter) .... (D)
Below left - BOOTS. Green transfer. (Black transfer lid.) c.1890-1930. (8 cms high) .... (C)
Below centre - BYNOL. Black transfer. Early C20th. (13 cms high) .... (C)
Below right - PATERSON'S. Brown transfer. Early C20th. (13 cms high) .... (C)

GAMES

PROMOTIONALS

Above - WILL'S'S. Black with raised brown lettering, plastic dominoes. Brown and cream tin. c.1930's. (16.5 cms long tin) .... (D)

Many items have been produced that carry company advertising but are not products of that company. These often useful, sometimes decorative mementoes are described here as promotionals.

Not all are either collectable or tangible.

Public buildings such as the Tate Gallery were endowed from company funds while sponsorship of sporting events and the arts is currently actively encouraged by government.

However, many promotionals were made specifically for collectors and issued in series with products to which dedicated brand loyalty was required. Several golly stickers were needed for each badge.

Utensils, games and toys which carried advertising may have been sold cheaply or given away free but it is interesting that some promotional clothing has a cachet which allows its sale price to be high. With souvenir 'T'shirts from pop concerts or films, fans pay to become advertisers.

Short thematic advertising campaigns have not affected the design of the more enduring promotionals such as bar games

Below - PLAYER'S. Red and black impressed ivorine dice. c.1930's .... (A)

Below - WILL'S'S. Orange, green, blue and white printed tin. c.1930. (15 cms wide) .... (D)

GAMES

Above - FRANKLYN'S. Red, white and black printed tin. c. 1920. (26 cms wide) .... (D)

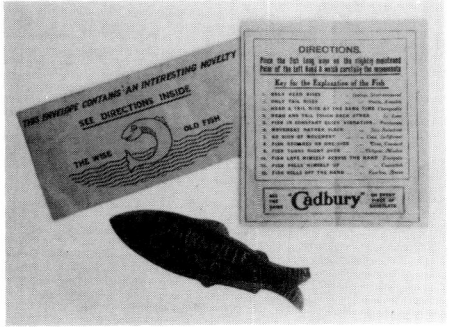

Above - BOURNVILLE passion indicator. c. 1935. (11.5 cm wide envelope) .... (A)

Above - FRANKLYN'S. Red, white and black printed tin. c. 1920. (22 x 38 cms) .... Rare (E)

but they have inspired some entertaining ephemera like the memorable 'Put a Tiger in Your Tank' tie-on tails and royal or major sporting occasions have produced everything from fitness guides to paper crowns. Unlike many items illustrated in this book, it is hard to imagine this source of collectables ever drying up.

Above - CAPSTAN. Mottled, dark brown, bakelite. 1930's. (23 cms wide) .... (C)

GAMES MARKERS

Above - CROWN CORK. Multi-coloured tin. c.1910. (15 cms wide) ....(D)

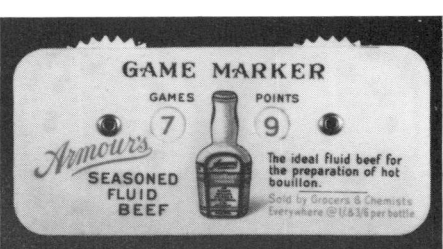

Left - ARMOUR'S. Red, blue and black on white celluloid. c.1930. (7.5 cms wide)............................(C)

Below left - OWBRIDGE'S. Multi-coloured card. c. 1920. (15 cms wide)... (C)

Below right - EDME. Black and red on cream celluloid. Made USA. c. 1910. (8 cms wide).......................... (C)

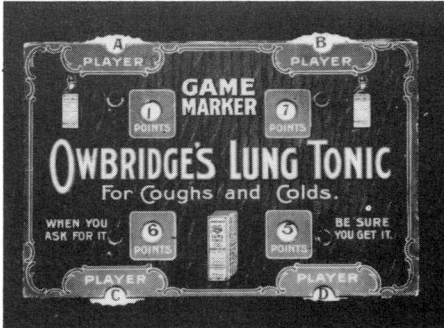

PLAYING CARDS

Above - SHELL. Multi-coloured. c.1920 .... (D)

Above - MASTERS'. Multi-coloured. c.1930 .... (D)

Printed playing cards first became fashionable in Europe in the fourteenth century but cards with advertising backs were not produced until the late nineteenth century. As individual cards are easily damaged or lost, a pack's value is greatly affected by its condition.

Below - SHIP. Red, black and yellow. c.1930 .... (D)

Below - PLAYER'S. Sepia red. c.1950 .... (B)

BOOKMARKS

Left - PLAYER'S. Red, white and blue with red ribbon. c.1930. (17 cms long) .... (B)
Centre - G.W.R. Grey, white and yellow. c.1910. (16.5 cms long) .... (C)
Right - NORTHERN ASSURANCE. Sepia on textured beige card. (City view on reverse.) 1909. (18 cms long) (C)

BOOKMARKS

Printed paper bookmarks, which date from the mid nineteenth century, have attracted a curious range of advertisers probably dominated by investment and insurance companies targeting the more affluent and respectable book buying public.

Left - EAMES. Sepia on cream. Price list on reverse. 'Shingling or Bobbing 2s. 0d.' c.1928. (18 cms long) .... (B)
Centre - SCOTTISH WIDOWS'. Blue on cream. 1914. (15.2 cms long)(B)
Right - PEARS'. Multi-coloured. On reverse - 'Sir Eramus Wilson, F. R. S., ... wrote: Pears' soap is a Balm for the Skin.' c.1888. (18.5 cms long) .... (D)

INKWELLS

RELIANCE. Black transfer on white. c.1910. (7.5 cms high) .... (D)

BLACKWOOD. Black transfer on white body. c.1890. (6.5 cms high) .... (F)

Possibly the earliest advertising inkwell, inscribed, 'Made at New Canton. 1751', was produced by the Bow factory and is owned by the Victoria and Albert Museum. Collectors looking for later examples will find few of these once common artefacts have survived and some, catalogued as inkwells, were designed as pen wipers such as the Blackwood's illustrated.

PERRY. Stoneware. Rare bird feeder type. Mid C19th. (11 cms high) ....(G)

WESTERN NEWS. Etched glass with metallic rim. c.1930. (11 cms diameter) .... (D)

OFFICE SUPPLIES

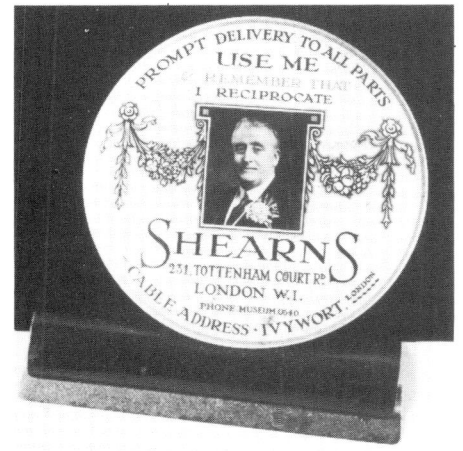 

SHEARNS. Badge type, bull dog clip. Sepia on cream. c.1930. (5 cms diameter) .... (A)

HARZER. Bull dog clip with grey on cream badge. c.1908. (3.2 cms diameter) .... (B)

Above - WILKINSON'S. Combined ruler and blotter. Black on cream celluloid. c.1925. .... (A)
Below - C.W.S. Black on yellow tin plate. c.1940. .... (A)

Below- Printed tin pencil sharpeners. L. to R. - VIROL. Dark blue, red and white. c.1925. C.W.S. POLISH. Black and grey. c.1930. C.W.S. Red and yellow. c.1930. C.W.S. PAINTS. Multi-coloured. c.1930. (All 2.5 cms high). (D)

POCKET MIRRORS

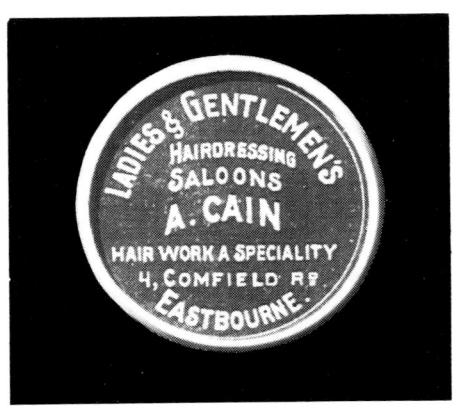

Above - A. CAIN. Metal rim. c.1910. ....(B)
Right - MILWARD'S. Plastic covered. c.1930's. ....(B)

Above - MORRISS. Metal rim. c.1910. ....(B)
Left - PETRALINE. Plastic covered. c.1930's. ....(B)

Above - PRIMA. Metal rim. c.1910. ....(B)
Right - PHILIPS. Plastic covered. c.1930's. ....(B)

BOTTLE OPENERS

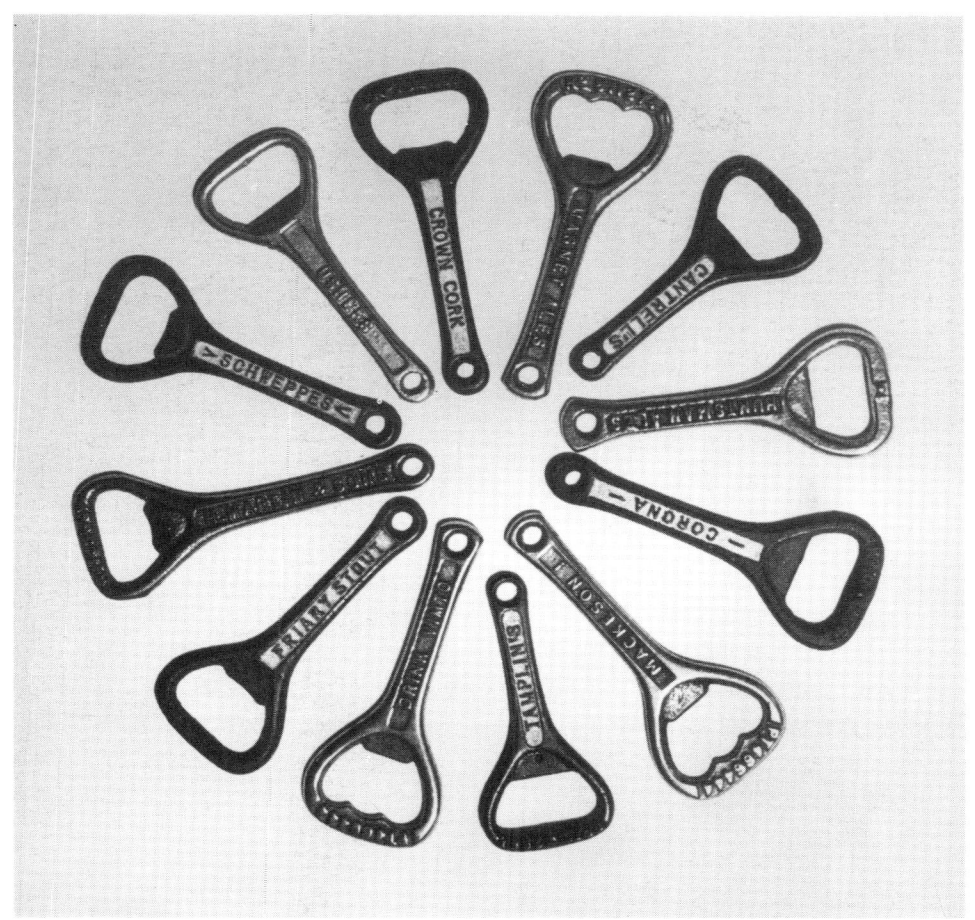

A collection of crown openers illustrating the interesting variations in design to be found in the most mundane of functional objects. 1895 - 1930's. (7 to 9 cms long) ....(A)

Every kitchen drawer had one, every bar and pantry had one and many pockets carried one. Bottle openers were indispensable for crown cork closures which were originally patented in Britain in 1892 for an American, William Painter. Late that decade, the Crown Cork Company, the original manufacturers, produced huge numbers of the crimped tin tops which compressed a thin disc of cork onto the bottle to create a good seal. (With the tin outside and the cork inside they made excellent pullover badges).

Three basic opener shapes exist: the claw (found in pocket knives), the pressed strip that also opens cans and the stirrup shape. Several patents cover minor variations of the stirrup, round tops being earliest and the plated dating from the late 1930's.

CALENDARS

CEYLINDO TEA. Multi-coloured. 1908. (50 x 72 cms) ....(E)

RANSON. Multi-coloured. 1898. (54 x 70 cms) ....(D)

FRISBY'S. Multi-coloured. 1912. (48 x 74 cms) ....(E)

PEARL ASSURANCE. Two tone brown and gold. 1914. (33 x 23 cms) ....(D)

CALENDARS

HICKS. Multi-coloured. (Printed by Alf Cooke.) 1904. (50 x 76 cms) .... (E)

SMITHSON. Black, madder, red and gold. (Alf Cooke.) 1891. (50 x 72 cms) .... (D)

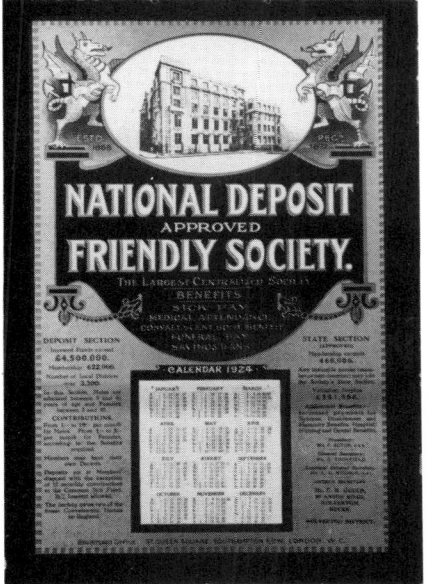

NATIONAL DEPOSIT. Two tone green, blue, black, white and sepia. 1924. (40 x 28 cms) .... (D)

SMITHSON. Black, madder, green and gold. (Alf Cooke.) 1892. (50 x 72 cms) .... (D)

POSTCARDS

Left to right - CARTER'S. Multi-coloured. c.1916. ....(D
WHEELER & WILSON. Multi-coloured. Postmarked 1911. ....(D
COLLEEN. Multi-coloured. c.1910. ....(C

The potential use of open cards as miniature travelling placards was realised by advertisers as soon as the special postage offer of half letter rate was made in 1869. However, the British Post Office retained restrictive control over the printing of postcards until 1899, so most early pictorial examples are continental. In 1902 it was accepted that both message and address could be put on one side of a card leaving the other side free for illustrations which rapidly made the picture postcard into a collecting craze.

Below, left to right - JOB WRAGG'S. Black and white photograph. c.1930. ....(B)
WATSON'S. Multi-coloured. c.1905. .... If in mint condition (D)
WESTGATE-ON-SEA. Multi-coloured. Fold out view card. c.1930. ....(C)

POSTCARDS

Below left - JU-VIS. Black and red. c.1910. ....(C)
Below right - C.W.S. SOAPS. Sepia photographic print. c.1930. ....(C)

Above left - CITY MEAT. Multi-coloured. c.1930. ....(C)
Above right - BISHOP & SONS. Multi-coloured. c.1905. ....(D)

Recently revived interest has been supported by many price guides which catalogue advertising as a collecting theme. As with showcards and tins, chromolithographic printing produced the most attractive examples and cards of this type reproducing poster advertisements generally attract the highest prices although condition is extremely important.

Below left - NESTLÉ'S. Multi-coloured. Postmarked 1903. ....(D)
Below right - CHILVERN. Multi-coloured. c.1920. ....(D)

SHOE HORN & BUTTON HOOKS

Above - REEVES. Metal shoe horn made in Germany. c.1910. (16.5 cms long) ....(A)

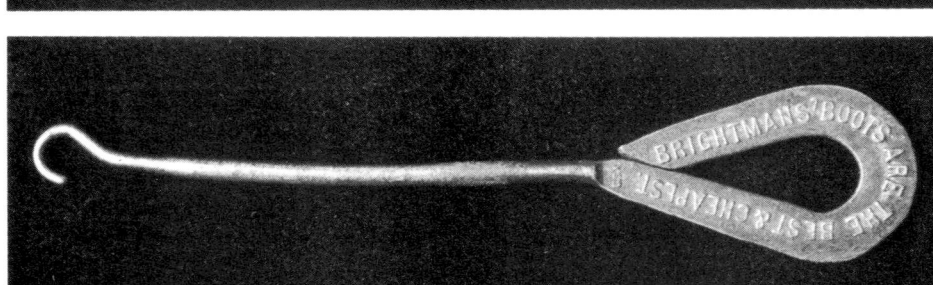

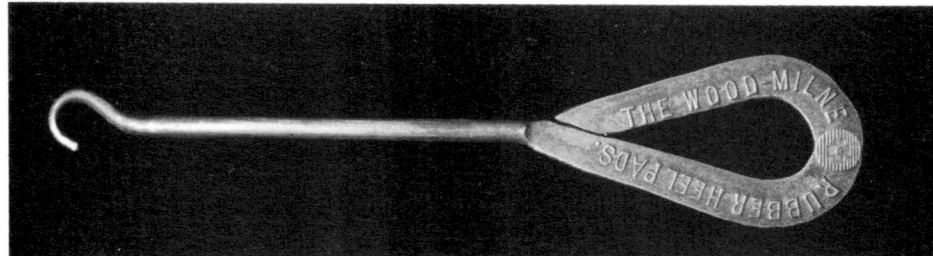

Button hooks
Top - ROBINSON. Made in Germany. c.1910. (11 cms long) ....(B)
Centre - BRIGHTMANS'. Made in USA. c. 1910. (13.2 cms long) ....(B)
Bottom - WOOD-MILNE. c.1910. (14 cms long) ....(A)

BADGES & MEDALLIONS

Above - A selection of post World War II promotional badges. ....(A)
Developed in the 1890's by patentees, Whitehead and Hoag, the tin badge, with its artwork protected by transparent celluloid, has remained a popular advertising novelty. Victorian badges were imported but Sanders, Fattorini and White and Lambert began production in this country early this century.

Below - BARRATT. Gold, red, white and black printed tin. 1897. (5.5 cms wide)...............................(C)

Below - JOHNSTON'S. Stamped brass. 1887. (4 cms wide)..(D)

POTTERY

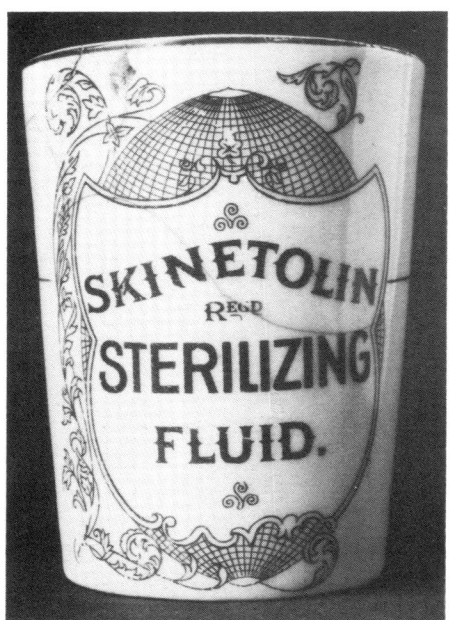

Above - SKINETOLIN. Sepia transfer on white body. c.1890. (10.5 cms high) Undamaged.....................(E)

Above - VIGORAL. Brown, green and pink with gold lustre lining on white body. c.1920. (9 cms high).....(C)

Below - HOVENDEN'S. Hard paste, white body shaving mug. Red and brown transfer; gold lustre lining; yellow, blue and red hand painting. c.1900. (11 cms high). Extremely rare......................................(F)

POTTERY

Above - ST. JULIEN. Multi-coloured, transfer printed tin. c.1950. (19 cms diameter)..................................(B)

Above right - CLARKE. Sepia transfer on white. c.1850. (14 cms diameter)......................................(E)

Right - HAYFIELD. Black screen printed transfer on white. c.1955. (13.5 cms wide)...............................(A)

Below - CADBURY'S. Transfer print with red, blue and yellow hand painted enamel colours. Saucer marked J & G Meakin. Cup marked Wedgewood & Co. Ltd.. c.1932. (saucer 14 cms diameter, cup 5.5 cms high) ....(D)

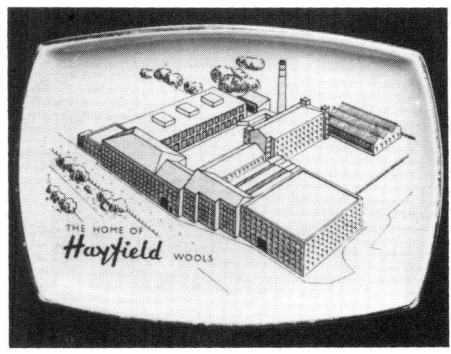

Below - MABEY. Brown transfer with enamel colours. Marked Copeland Spode. c.1950. (17 cms diameter) ....(C)

113

INSERTS

OTHER EPHEMERA

Above, left to right - WHITELEY'S. Multi-coloured. c.1890. (15 x 9 cms) ....(C)
MAYPOLE. Multi-coloured. c.1900. (12 x 8 cms) ....(C)
SUNLIGHT. Multi-coloured. c.1900. (10 x 17 cms) ....(C)

Left - SMITH'S. Multi-coloured. c.1910. (14 x 9 cms) ....(C)

Bottom left - SKIPPERS. Multi-coloured. c. 1905. (14 x 9 cms..(D)

Below - LUX. Multi-coloured. c.1900. (14 x 12 cms) ....(C)

MECHANICALS

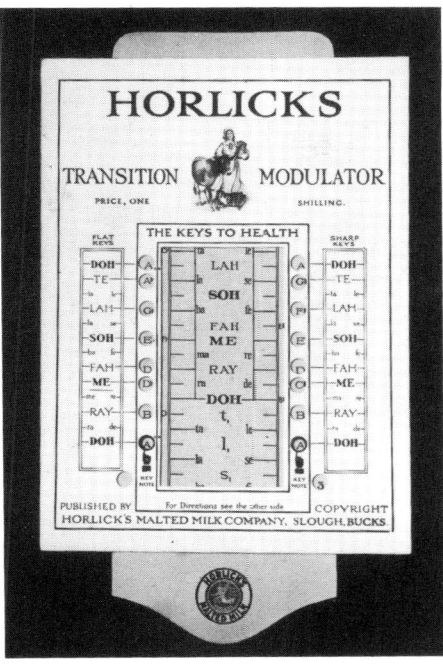

Above - HORLICKS. White with blue printing. Blue and red on beige insert. c. 1930. (22.5 x 8 cms) .... (C)

Below - BOVRIL. Blue with black printing. Black on white insert. c.1930. (8.8 x 14 cms folded) .... (C)

Above - OXO. Multi-coloured. Designed so the child's arm can be raised seemingly in order to pour Oxo all down her chequered napkin. c.1930. (8 x 11 cms) ....(C)

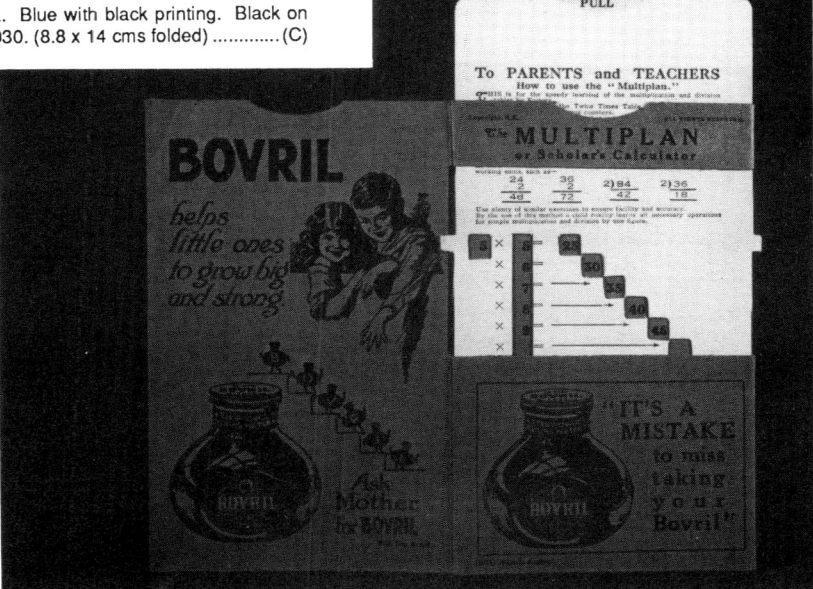

BILLHEADS

Top - KINMOND. Black print on white. Marked 1914. (20 cms wide) ....(B)
Centre - ROYAL DAYLIGHT. Two tone blue on white. c.1920. (22 cms wide) ....(B)
Below - SCHWEPPES. Blue on white. 1908. (21 cms wide) ....(B)

BILLHEADS

Above - ZEBRA. Red, black and yellow on white. c.1910. (13 cms wide) ....(B)
Centre - WHEATLEY & BATES. Black and red on white. c.1910. (21 cms wide) ....(B)
Bottom - THREE TORCHES. Blue, red and mauve on white. c.1910. (13.5 cms wide) .... (B)

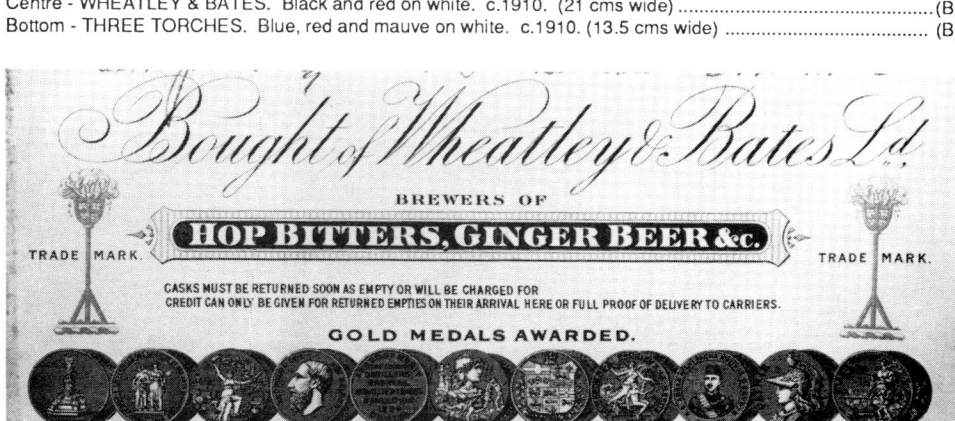

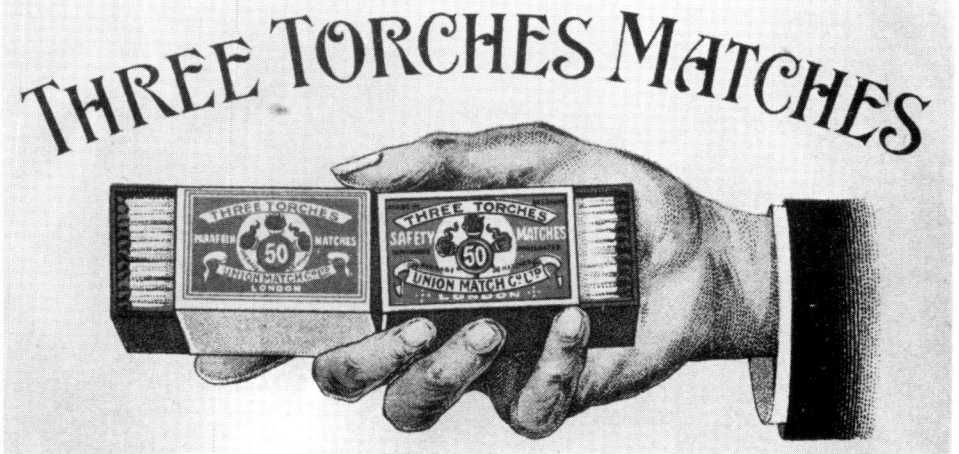

PLACES TO VISIT

Most local, city and shire museums are worth investigating. Besides being displayed individually, interesting items of advertising are often used as set dressing. Annual bottle shows and the National Collectors' Fairs are also good places for seeing exhibitions of advertising collectables as well as for buying them.

ALFORD, Lincolnshire. Manor House Folk Museum. (Dairy and period shops.)

BATTLE, East Sussex. Buckley's Shop Museum. (Period shops.)

BEAUMARIS, North Wales. Museum of Childhood. (Tin money boxes.)

BRAMBER, West Sussex. House of Pipes. (Arcade of tobacconists.)

BURTON-ON-TRENT, Staffordshire. Bass Museum of Brewing.

CRICH, Derbyshire. Tramway Museum. (Enamels.)

DUDLEY, West Midlands. Black Country Museum. (Signs.)

DUNDEE, Scotland. Spalding Golf Museum.

GLOUCESTER, 'The Pack Age.' The Robert Opie Collection.

HEREFORD. Museum of Cider.

LONDON. Museum of London. (Period shops.)
　　　　　Heritage Motor Museum, Syon Park.
　　　　　London Toy and Model Museum. (Figural tins).
　　　　　Victoria and Albert Museum. (Franklin biscuit tin collection.)

NORWICH, Norfolk. Colman's Mustard Shop and Museum.

READING, Berkshire. Museum and Art Gallery. (Huntley and Palmer collection.)

ROCHDALE, Lancashire. Toad Lane Museum. (C.W.S. history.)

ST. HELENS, Merseyside. Pilkington Glass Museum. (Bottles.)

SHEFFIELD PARK, East Sussex. Bluebell Railway Museum. (Signs.)

SHUGBOROUGH, Staffordshire. Museum of Rural Staffordshire. (Signs.)

STANLEY, County Durham. Beamish Open Air Museum. (Signs.)

WOODSTOCK, Oxfordshire. County Museum. (Period shops.)

YORK. Castle Museum. (Period shops.)

BIBLIOGRAPHY

Various specialist groups such as the Ephemera Society and the Street Jewellery Society publish newsletters. 'Collectors Mart', first published in 1980 under the title of 'Finders Keepers', is the magazine for news and events.

ANDERSON & SWINGLEHURST. 'Ephemera of Travel and Transport'. New Cavendish. 1981.
ASKEY, D. 'Stoneware Bottles'. Bowman Graphics. 1981.
BAGLEE & MORLEY. 'Street Jewellery'. New Cavendish. 1978.
BAGLEE & MORLEY. 'More Street Jewellery'. New Cavendish. 1982.
BEAVER, P. 'The Match Makers'. Henry Melland. 1985.
BECK, D. 'The Bottle Collecting Book'. Hamlyn. 1973.
CLARK, H. M. 'The Tin Can Book'. New American Library. 1977.
COVILL Jr., W. E. 'Ink Bottles and Ink Wells'. Sullwold. 1971.
DALE, R. 'The Price Guide to Black and White Pot-Lids'. Antique Collectors' Club. 1977.
DEMPSEY, M. 'Pipe Dreams'. Pavilion. 1982.
EVANS & LAWSON. 'A Nation of Shopkeepers'. Plexus. 1981.
FRANKLIN, M. J. 'British Biscuit Tins, 1868-1939'. New Cavendish. 1979.
FRANKLIN, M. J. 'British Biscuit Tins'. V & A Museum. 1984.
FRESCO-CORBU. 'Vesta Boxes'. Lutterworth. 1983.
GREEN, R. 'A Treasury of British Bottles'. Old Bottles and Treasure Hunting. 1982.
GRIFFITH, D. 'Decorative Printed Tins'. Studio Vista. 1979.
HEDGES, A. A. 'Collecting Bottles'. Shire. 1975.
HINDLEY, D. & G. 'Advertising in Victorian England. 1837-1901'. Wayland. 1972.
JACKSON, W. A. 'The Victorian Chemist and Druggist'. Shire. 1981.
LANDER & DANIEL. 'The True Story of H. P. Sauce'. Methuen. 1985.
LITHERLAND. 'Bottle Collecting'. MAB Publishing.
LUKINS, J. 'Doulton Burslem Advertising Wares'. Venta. 1985.
MORGAN, R. 'The Benign Blue Coffin'. Kollectarama. 1978.
NEVETT, T. R. 'Advertising in Britain. A History'. Heinemann. 1982.
OPIE, R. 'Rule Britannia'. Viking. 1985.
OPIE, R. 'The Art of the Label'. Simon and Schuster. 1987.
OSBORNE, K. 'Bygone Breweries'. Rochester Press. 1982.
PRESTON, G. 'Advertising'. Batsford. 1971.
RICCI, F. M. 'Biscuits'. Cino Del Duco. 1982.
SCHOFIELD & KAMM. 'Lager Lovelies'. Richard Drew. 1984.
SETCHFIELD, F. R. 'The Official Badge Collector's Guide'. Longman. 1986.
TRESISE, C. E. 'Tavern Treasures'. Blandford. 1983.
VINCE, J. 'Fire Marks'. Shire. 1973.
VINCENZI, P. 'Taking Stock'. Willow. 1985.
de VRIES, L. & LAVER, J. 'Victorian Advertisements'. Murray. 1968.
WILLIAMS, E. 'The Story of Sunlight Soap'. Unilever. 1984.
WILLS, G. 'English Glass Bottles'. John Bartholomew. 1974.
WILSON, K. 'Commemorative Breweriana'. Keith Wilson. 1985.
WORTHINGTON & WILLIAMS. 'Automobilia'. Batsford and RAC. 1979.

SPECIALIST MAGAZINES AND BOOKS FOR SPECIALIST COLLECTORS.

BBR Publishing, 2 Strafford Avenue, Elsecar, Nr Barnsley, S Yorks, S74 8AA, England

MR. BULWARK

MR. WOODBINE

MISS

MASTER LEGATION

MRS. BULWARK

MASTE

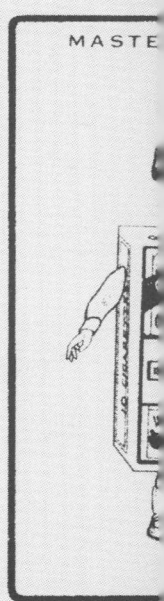